Get Your Real Estate Strategies for Your Real Estate Investing Life

Table of Contents

Preface 1
Chapter : 1 The Need for a Real Estate Strategy 3
   Preamble 3
   Why Should You Have a Strategy in the First Place? 5
   Strategy and Routine 8
Chapter : 2 Choosing the Perfect Real Estate Investment Strategy 11
   Benefits of Owning Real Estate Property 12
   Crafting a Real Estate Investment Strategy 16
   Ways to Achieve Your Goal 17
   Strategies to Consider When Investing in Real Estate 19
   Short-Term Versus Long-Term Real Estate Investments .. 23
   Long-Term Strategies 23
   Short-Term Real Estate Investments 24
   Niches to Explore as an Investor 26
   The Importance of Finding Your Real Estate Niche 27
   Tips to Find the Perfect Niche 28
   Debunking the Passive Income Myth 30
   What to Delegate Based on Experience 33
   Are You Ready to Invest Yet? 34
   Knowledge is Power When It Comes to Real Estate Investment 36
Chapter : 3 Real Estate Investment Mistakes 40

Chapter : 4 Real Estate Investment Strategies 57
   Rental Properties 57
   Flipping Houses 61
   The Process of Flipping Houses 62
   Barriers to Flipping Houses 64
   Sources of Finance When Flipping Houses 65
   The Pros and Cons of Property Flipping 66
   Wholesaling Real Estate 68
   How Does the Deal Work? 69
   Mistakes that Wholesalers Make 71
   Benefits of Wholesaling Real Estate 72
   Disadvantages of Wholesaling Real Estate 74
   Automatic Entrances Make Life Easier for You 75
   Delegation is Still Vital 75

Chapter : 5 Leverage in Real Estate Investments 76
   The Mindset of the Successful Real Estate Investor 77
   Delegation 82
   Real Estate Brokers 82
   Who Is a Broker? 82
   How to Choose the Best Real Estate Broker 83
   Advantages of Hiring a Real Estate Broker 85
   Disadvantages of Working with a Broker 88
   Banks and Real Estate Loans 88
   The Process of Getting a Bank Loan 89
   What Do You Need to Qualify for a Bank Loan? 90
   Benefits of Bank Loans 91

Disadvantages of Investment Loans 92
Private Real Estate Investment 93
Institutional vs. Retail Investments: What Is the Difference?
.... 93

Chapter : 6 95
Looking Into the Future 95
What are Goals? 95
Why Do You Need Goals? 96
Steps to Come Up with Perfect Goals 97
Barriers to Goal Setting for Investors 99
Long-Term Versus Short-Term Goals 101
Short-Term Goals 101
Long-Term Goals 103
Evaluation of Goals for Refinement and to Establish Effectiveness 105
What is Evaluation? 106
When to Modify Your Goals 108
Return on Investment in Real Estate 110
How to Evaluate the Performance 110

Chapter : 7 Understanding Real Estate Investment Risks and Risk Management 112
Risks in Real Estate Investment 112
Why Is Real Estate Risk More Complicated Than Other Asset Classes? 115
Causes of Risk in Real Estate Investment 115
Risk Management Process in Real Estate Investments 117

Real Estate Taxes 120

Real Estate Tax Assessment 122

Top Tax Mistakes That You Need to Avoid 123

Are Your Real Estate Assets Protected? 125

Bonus Chapter   Preface to the 3rd book "Potential of Real Estate Rentals.. 127

Preface

A lot of millionaires have gained wealth through investing in real estate. Every wage worker will tell you one thing: no one gets rich from working a day job where they pay you wages. When you use the money you have, you get the capacity to grow. Additionally, you can use other people's money to make your own. This book tells you how to invest in real estate and points you in the right direction when it comes to getting finances.

It is not all about buying a property at little to nothing – the issue is all about buying a property and then selling it off at a profit. The profit is not all about the selling price and the buying price but all about the costs you incur as well. We will discuss all these in the book.

What about the risks that you come across that end up making the process miserable? You cannot avoid risk altogether in any real estate transaction, but all you need to know what to do so that you reduce this risk.

Who this book is for?

Are you an investor that does not know where to start from in terms of real estate investing? This is the perfect book to introduce you to the different concepts and allow you to forge forward with confidence. Whether a newbie or a seasoned investor, this book has something for you.

Chapter : 1
The Need for a Real Estate Strategy

Preamble

Real estate investing gives you more than something to do as a developer—you get to enjoy what you put in, and then you make profits. The value of real estate investments cannot be overlooked, with many moguls attributing their success to real estate. Investing in real estate has become one of the sure strategies for you to enjoy as an investor. Though it takes time and some money, you end up making more profits if you do things right.

This is why you need to have a strategy in place. The strategy guides you on what to do and what to avoid and it gives you the right direction to follow to make sure you succeed. Let us look at the comparison:

Buyer's Market		Seller's Market
The supply of property is high compared to willing buyers on the market. The ideal scenario is the supply being higher than demand by customers. Supply > Demand	Vs	Here, the supply of property is low compared to willing buyers in the market. The ideal situation is the demand is more than the supply. Demand > Supply

You need to understand both the buyer's and the seller's market when you jump into real estate.

Before we look at the strategy in details, we need to look at the factors that make real estate a good market to invest in.

- *Technology and Real Estate Investment.* We cannot talk about real estate investments without talking about the role of technology in the whole setup. Advancements in technology have led to rapid changes in the industry, and with this, investors need to adapt rapidly to the changes to maximize exposure of their properties.

Under technology, we have the blockchain, which is now a reality of this industry. Blockchain technology is changing the way investors interact with the market as well as the property they have interest in. The real estate market is changing, and we also need to do the same.

- *High Demand for Homes.* With the demand for homes on the rise, indeed, home prices might also rise. This means that you will gain more if you decide to invest in a home. The average home price has grown over the past few years by up to 10% per year. This means that if you decide to invest in real estate, you will gain between 5% and 10% in profits.

- *Millennials Buying Homes.* Statistics show that this age group is increasingly buying home after home. Most of them are going after luxury homes on the market, and they make decisions faster than other buyers due to the capacity to access loans.

Apart from the millennial, single families are also purchasing homes daily. This has led to the development of single-family rental homes.

In all these, one thing remains static: the need for the right strategy. With the best strategy, you can have what you need in terms of real estate investment.

Why Should You Have a Strategy in the First Place?

Before you can even go ahead to understand how a business strategy can help your business, you first need to ask yourself whether you have one in place. Many real estate investors don't have one, and they even don't know what to do for the future.

A real estate investment strategy is all about setting goals for your business and coming up with a plan to achieve the goals. Developing a long-term business strategy involves where you are at the moment, determining where you need to be in the future, and how you will get there. The strategy can be any document that works for you; it can be a written document or a digital one.

Whether you are starting in real estate or you are an astute developer, you will achieve a few benefits:

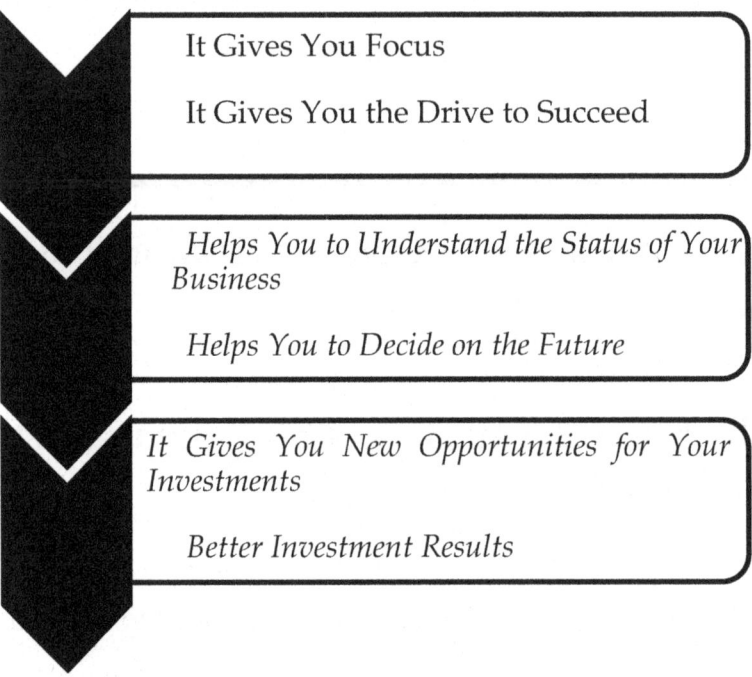

Chart: Summary of the benefits of investing in real estate

- It gives you focus. With a strategy in place, you are always clear of the current status of the business and where you are heading to. This makes your goals clear and gives you the direction you need to that you align the business to achieve your business strategy.

Many investors leave their businesses to drift along without any purpose whatsoever. At the end of it all, they find out that they cannot compute their profits; they don't know what they spend along the way and can't even know what each property brought in term of profits.

- *It gives you the drive to succeed.* When you have a strategy in place, you give your team the stimulus to perform at their best and take your business where it ought to be.

With goals to meet and proper plans set down to get to the goals, the team has a clear path to achieve these goals.

- *It helps you to understand the status of your business.* Before you can come up with a long-term strategy, you need first to understand where you are at the moment. This involves looking at your business, generally including the primary drivers, including the performance of the real estate properties that you own. You also need to consider the weaknesses, strengths, and threats associated with each property that you hold. This gives you a snapshot of the market so that you can move ahead better.

- *It helps you to decide on the future.* With a business strategy in place, you get to come up with a long-term vision and what you wish to achieve, say, in 5 years to come. You might be looking for a way to grow your profitability by a certain percentage or to increase value for your business.
- *It gives you new opportunities for your investments.* When you review and work on your real estate investment strategy, you go through a process that allows you to come up with new ideas that you might not have identified any other way.

You also get to step back into the business and re-look at the business before coming up with the best results. You might find out that you have enough funds to invest in other properties to diversify your portfolio.

- *It gives better investment results.* With a real estate investment strategy, you stand to achieve better business performance because you are focused on business success. With the strategy directing you, it is easy to go where you want to be.

Strategy and Routine

Many traders have one mistake that they do over and over again: the routine. Many investors found themselves stuck in a rut, whereby they do the daily tasks the same way each day, contributing little to the overall goals of the strategy.

They might deem the tasks to be miniscule, but they form important parts of the whole system that cannot be done away with completely.

Remember that as you run your investments, you have competition from other investors that might be interested in the same properties as you. Towards this end, you end up performing essential tasks that include:

- Wake up and follow the leads that you have not closed over the past and try to close them.
- Look for motivated sellers that have a deal that you can take up.
- Look for more funds to allow you to buy more properties.

Along with this, you have to contend with hundreds of ideas, tactics, and strategies that you have to tackle each day. This can be overwhelming if you don't have a strategy in place.

With routine comes to lack of movement in your business. The ability to know where to go and what to do next is defined by the right strategy.

Through real estate investing, you can increase the net worth to a great level. You will reach your goals faster than ever, and you get to preserve your wealth for retirement. Many people have done this without a lot of capital, to begin with.

It remains a fact that if you want to build and preserve wealth no matter where you are and where you live, then you need to go into real estate.

The demand for real estate in many areas remains constant though there are a lot of factors that influence the demand. The best news is that even when the economy isn't stable, you will always get good opportunities because this is the time to buy properties at low prices.

The secret to building wealth via real estate is being able to understand the changes in the market and the pressures, then trying to capitalize on any opportunities that come up. With real estate, you are always assured of a steady supply of buyers who have an interest in the property that you have.

Chapter : 2
Choosing the Perfect Real Estate Investment Strategy

From a statistical perspective, the act of investing in real estate is a bit similar to investing in securities because for you to profit, you must establish the value of the properties and make a lot of guesses about how much you expect in return.

For many people, the easiest way to get wealth is to inherit it from their parents. Another good way is to marry a spouse with wealth. The third and most obvious choice is to invest in real estate.

Those millionaires you read about have a history of real estate. With the current economy, even when both husband and wife are working full-time jobs, it is hard to accumulate much wealth. Having real estate investments give you enough wealth to live comfortably and even send your kids to school.

In search of sure wealth, many people watched the financial channels, bought financial papers, and went ahead to invest in the stock market. In doing this, they put their future in the hands of others rather than trying to have their future in their own hands. When trading stocks, we learned that the prices could go down, but it isn't essential that they go down again as you expect. From stock trading, we also found out that many corporate managers were more concerned with enriching themselves and forgot about the investors.

On the other hand, real estate investments are different from stock investments because you have all the control. You make the decisions that affect your future and stick to them. When you trade in real estate, you determine the kind of purchases or sales that meet your goals.

Benefits of Owning Real Estate Property

There are various benefits to owning real estate property.

- *It allows you to build equity.* One of the benefits of real estate investing is that you can build equity. As you pay off the mortgage associated with the property, you build equity. With equity, you get the leverage that allows you to buy more properties so that you increase cash flow.

You can use it to take out loans when the terms are favorable, then use the funds for other investment projects.

- *You can enjoy the passive income.* Once you acquire real estate investments, you don't have to be actively involved in the investments; they work for you even when sleeping. With several real estate investment properties, you are sure that you can generate income to pay off various expenses and have profits.

This type of investment allows you to do what you enjoy instead of spending all the time at work.

- *You have a steady income.* A properly selected rental property gives you constant income in the form of monthly payments. When you invest in real estate, you have more control over any risks, even with the threat of market slumps.

The income increases in value as time goes by due to the appreciation of the property. However, you cannot predict the value of the investment, but you are sure that you won't end up with losses.

The potential for earning a high rate of return on investments is high. With real estate investment, you are looking at a potential return of between 10% and 20%; however, this depends on the prevailing market conditions as well as the location of the property.

It is even more profitable if you have longer leases on the property. This is especially true if you opt for commercial real estate as opposed to residential properties.

- *Inflation is on your side.* As the population grows, the demand for housing also increases. When this happens, the demand pushes up the rental prices, especially when the supply isn't keeping up with demand.
- *You can enjoy the benefits of portfolio diversion.* If you are looking for a way to diversify, then you need to invest in a physical asset. Investing in real estate gives you a tangible asset that you can always monetize via renting, and you can make money regardless of the prevailing market conditions.

The real estate investment market is more resilient against changes in market prices compared to stocks or bonds. With real estate, you can have the stability you need to diversify your portfolio.

- *It protects you against inflation.* Many traders cannot even think about inflation, but this isn't the case with real estate investors. To shield yourself against inflation, you need to have an investment that will stay true even with changing conditions.

Real estate investment protects you against both the long-term and short-term effects of inflation.

- *It allows you to enjoy tax benefits.* Real estate investment provides you with tax benefits that reduce the costs of running the investment. It also increases your profits.
- *Real estate generates wealth.* You can generate wealth through building equity, appreciation, and shielding against inflation.
- *The value appreciates over time.* Since time immemorial, many traders have invested in real estate knowing that they will be able to return their investment in a few years. The value of real estate investments increases due to various reasons. First, the rental rates grow due to the demand for rental houses and the high construction costs. Secondly, the demand for high-end houses makes more people bid for higher prices, which make the value increase.
- *It reduces the level of risks.* One of the reasons many traders opt for real estate investments compared to others is because it helps to mitigate risks. Having a static income each month is a good investment, but having the shield against higher levels of risk through real estate investment is a good idea.

The bottom line: With real estate investment, you have a good source for passive income. The demand for both commercial and residential property is on the rise, which means you can get profit from your investments. The properties make a great part of any investment portfolio as well.

Crafting a Real Estate Investment Strategy

The real estate is a multi-billion dollar industry allowing you to invest in various opportunities. However, just like any other business, you need to have a plan when approaching this industry. With the right strategies, you can unlock the success you need to make it as a trader.

Before you come up with the right strategy, you need to have a goal. A goal refers to something that you plan to achieve. In real estate investment, your goal might be to buy another investment property in a month or earn a certain amount of income per month from the property. Whatever the goal is, you need to make sure that it is something that you can achieve. You need to look at various elements.

- *The goal should be measurable.* The goal needs to be measurable. You should be able to include various limits. For instance, you can use a time limit to know what to achieve in such a time. Goals that don't have a definite limit are harder to achieve. A good example is to aim to achieve two units each year to add to what you already have.

- *The goal should be attainable.* It should be attainable and realistic; otherwise, you will soon shelve and never implement it. Goals shouldn't be too high such that you fail to achieve them.
- *The goal should evolve over time.* It needs to be modifiable to suit changing market conditions. With time, many things will change in the market, and when this happens, you need to make sure your goals can adapt to the changes.

After you set the goals, you need to know how to achieve it at the end of the day. Achieving your goal is not an easy feat as many people have come up with goals and failed to achieve them at the end of the day.

Ways to Achieve Your Goal

Here are a few components of achieving your goals:

1. *Clearly communicate the goals.* You need to bring out the goal clearly. Once you have the goal written down, go ahead and tell it to your friends, agent, attorney, family, and well, everyone. These people will keep on asking you about your promise and therefore push you to attain it. For most people, achieving goals is a team effort.

Yes, you can come up with the perfect goal—clearly defined, attainable, and measurable. What is left is to implement the goal.

If you share your written goal with the major players in your market, you will get many calls from them to bring you more opportunities only if they know that you are serious with what you are planning.

2. *Have milestone.* Once you have a clear goal, the next step is to lay out the plan to achieve this goal. This means you have to draft a plan so that you know when to achieve a specific milestone. These milestones are the ones that help you to achieve the goal. Once you come up with the milestones, make sure you communicate them to the people that you work with.

Here is a sample milestone for a budding real estate investor:

- Find and come up with the perfect team
- Evaluate the current market
- Identify a few great properties
- Evaluate the properties and choose the best
- Have a plan to handle the properties
- Come up with a budget
- Handle the properties

3. *Overcome obstacles.* Every business has obstacles that you need to overcome. For instance, you might hope to run your business in a month, but you find that it is taking you longer than you expected, requiring double the work and costs you more than you have ever thought. These are facts that you need to live with.
4. *Focus.* Goals are complicated, and it is a fact you need to live with. For many goals, the closer you are to achieving the goal, the more opportunities you discover. Many will seem better than the opportunities you are working with at the moment.

Well, the opportunities might be great and appealing, but don't let them steer you away from what you are going after. When you get distracted, you steer away from the goals and will slow down the pace of your growth.

Once you have the right goals, make sure you incorporate them in your strategy.

Strategies to Consider When Investing in Real Estate

- *Go for real estate properties in good neighborhoods.* For you to make money, you need to get real estate property in areas that are considered ideal. Go for a property that is in an area that many people wish to live. "Hot"

property is always in demand by many people, where the residents are in the high earning bracket, or it is in an area with good security and road networks.
- *Buy and hold.* If you are looking for long-term real estate investments, then this is the best strategy to use. Real estate property appreciates over time, which makes it the best when it comes to purchasing and holding on to it.

The premise of this strategy is that you buy a property then hold onto it for a very long period. In many cases, the aim is to take advantage of the increases in the prices in the future. In many markets, the price of real estate properties ends up doubling after a few years. Additionally, rental income tends to increase as the years go by, which means you enjoy more rental income with the years.

To get the best property for this strategy, you need to try and know more about the neighborhood, the market, and the costs of running the property. Such property requires positive cash flow; otherwise, you end up losing money. You can choose to manage the property on your own or hire property managers to do it for you.

There are different properties in this category—from entire apartments to single-family homes.

- *Fix and flip.* If you are in the market for active, short-term real estate investments, then this strategy is the best one for you. Here, you buy a property, renovate it, and then sell it off. However, you need to know how to identify the right property to flip. The best way to do this would be to consult a professional so you can identify any issues and avoid losing money on the trade.

When flipping the property, time becomes your biggest asset. The longer it takes for you to flip the property, the more money you end up paying in terms of expenses.

Also called renovation, this strategy requires you to put in some money towards renovating the property. It can be as simple as a new paint job or fitting a new carpet, or as complicated as changing the entire layout of the house or even adding an extension to the property.

- *Wholesaling.* This entails creating income without having to put in money. As a wholesaler, you find a seller that wishes to put up their property for sale and then you do it for him. You aim to sell the property then get a share of the selling price. For this to work, you need to have a reliable network with a database of sellers as well as lawyers.

- *Subdivision.* This works when you have a property that you subdivide into two chunks. Each of the chunks has its title. You can then go ahead to sell off a single block of the property, or you can develop it while the other block remains on its own.
- *Dual occupancy.* This works when you create more than one rental income from a single title. You do this by adding another flat to the back of the property or splitting an existing property to accommodate a tenant. This becomes profitable because you can sell it off at a higher value.
- *Development.* Here, you take the block of land, and then you build structures from scratch. You can build a single structure or several on the same piece of land. The only downside is that for these developments, you need to have more capital to pull it off.
- *Commercial real estate.* This is all about investing in real estate for commercial purpose. For this, you need a bigger deposit compared to residential investments. The good thing about this type of investment is that leases on the property are usually longer than other residential properties. Tenants can opt to sign leases that run for more than three years. This gives you bigger security on your income.

- *Buying land.* This strategy involves buying land without putting up any structure on it. You might not have income on the land unless you sell it off.

Short-Term Versus Long-Term Real Estate Investments

When you first get into the real estate investment market, you need to consider whether you want to go into it for the short term or the long term. Both of the strategies can give you profits, but each comes with its benefits and drawbacks.

Long-Term Strategies

You buy and then hold onto the property for the long term. Here, you rely on time and cash flow to be successful. The common strategies include:

- Buy and hold
- Using real estate investment trusts

Advantages: The long-term investment gives you positive cash flow, consistent income, and real estate appreciation. As you hold onto the property, you get to pay off the mortgage each month as you build up equity on the property. You enjoy high yields on your investment, liquidity, and enjoy passive income on your property. Additionally, you get to diversify your portfolio.

The value of the property will go up as you wait for the time to dispose of it. With the right investment decision, you will usually invest right. Over time, the property appreciates, and you end up winning at the end of the day.

This type of investment is not just for the long term—it is also about your future. Even if you don't have money in your account, you still have something that you can pass on to your children.

Disadvantages: Usually, you don't have the cash to pay for the property outright, which means you have to take out a loan. This results in debt for you.

Rental properties need upkeep. You have to be responsible for repairs as well as other expenses. Insurance and taxes can also take a toll on you, especially if you have many properties.

Short-Term Real Estate Investments

Also known as temporary investments, it comes with a short timeline, usually less than three years. Examples of this type of investment are fix, flip, and wholesaling.

Advantages:

- You get to earn profits faster, and you see the results of your efforts much quickly.
- You get some flexibility, which means you don't have to tie up your money in long term situations.
- You don't need in-depth knowledge of the market to succeed.

Disadvantages:

These investments are taxed differently compared to long term investments. This makes the rates higher than long-term taxes.

Holding onto the property for a short time makes you incur more expenses. For instance, you might end up paying more in terms of commissions to the agent. It might not be possible to earn interest on short-term investments.

For the strategy to survive the market and to give you the success you need, it is vital that you understand the various niches. Let us look at the real estate niches that you can invest in and what each brings for you.

Many traders focus on a single niche and try to get the best out of it.

Niches to Explore as an Investor

- *For Sale by Owner:* In most cases, the seller realizes that he can't market the home or has tried and failed. This is when they list the property with the agent.
- *Vacation Homes:* This can become a successful niche if the homes are located in an area that appeals to a lot of people. However, you need to be ready for high competition. Many of the homes need extensive advertisement to make sure you get the people to invest in it.
- *Commercial Properties:* Here, you are dealing in homes that you plan to rent out to other people to get rent. The main property in this category is properties that offer office space to the buyers.
- *Luxury Homes:* This is quite inviting at first, but many people end up making losses because they didn't come up with the best strategy. These properties need special marketing, which means you have to pay more in terms of advertisement costs.
- *Condominiums:* The popularity of condos has grown over the past few years, with many homeowners opting for these properties. Many of these owners use condominiums periodically, meaning you also have to be vigilant when advertising the condos.

- *First-Time Home Buyers:* With the right communication aspect, you might want to handle first time buyers. This group is more excited than the others to start the process of hunting for a house. The group represents nearly a third of buyers each year. While most of them have a limited budget, they are always in a hurry to close a deal, so expect them to go through the paces very fast.
- *Rental Properties:* This real estate market niche is ideal for those investors that have a full-time job on the side. Location is a huge aspect when it comes to choosing the ideal rental property. You also need to consider the family-size, whether single-family or multiple. The only way to make sure you are successful with this niche is to make sure the tenants are satisfied at all times.

The Importance of Finding Your Real Estate Niche

Every investor is looking for that special something to get leverage over other competitors. This is why you need to find the perfect niche to invest in. Once you know your niche, you can use technology to get more information and get to market yourself.

When it comes to investing in real estate, you need to be unique. Some investors do this by using colors and funny gimmicks—well, people remember them but for the wrong reasons. The best way to stand out is to create a brand in a niche. Doing this makes people identify you and will look for you when they decide to buy or sell.

When you find the ideal niche, you get to understand the type of clients you are dealing with. You will know their needs and how they desire to be fulfilled, and you will go ahead to do this. Marketing your properties will be easy and won't seem like a burden to you.

The investing strategy that you opt for needs to build itself into the marketing niche. This is explained in the book "Lear the Right Way Real Estate."

Tips to Find the Perfect Niche

1. *Analyze your options.* Remember that all niches might not be available in your region, which means that you need to identify the opportunities available in the area. Once you have a list of the options, you need to understand the ones that have the highest profitability.

The list will be dictated by a few issues that include the buyers of the homes and what types of properties are common in the area.

2. *Analyze the fit.* After you choose the options, the next step is to make sure that the niche you choose is a perfect fit for your investment options. Look at each niche and analyze it in such a way that you understand whether you will be comfortable handling the investment. Look at the capital needs, the level of effort you need to put in, and the returns so that you understand if it aligns with your goals.
3. *Your budget.* This is critical because you need to afford what you are planning to do. When it comes to investing in real estate, you need to be sure that you have the money to invest in, and even to cover losses. Take time to understand what each niche requires in terms of investment and payment of costs.
4. *Analyze your commitment.* Are you committed to the cause or you are just in to try the waters? Some investments take years to give you returns, and you need to be patient and committed to achieving this. If you are in a hurry, then go for short-term investments.
5. *Follow your heart.* To succeed in real estate, you need to have a passion for what you do. You need to have the

push to wake up each morning. The push shouldn't be just about the money—you might end up burning out.

Go for a niche that will give you fulfillment. For instance, if you love space, then it makes a lot of sense to buy land and develop it yourself.

6. *Make it official.* Once you pinpoint a few niches, you need to make yourself more professional by getting certified. Getting certified is another way to grow your reputation in the desired niche. Certification gives you access to various networks; it allows you to have opportunities to build networks and create fruitful relationships.

Debunking the Passive Income Myth

One of the reasons many investors take to real estate investments is to enjoy passive income. This myth has made many investors buy properties, and then hire property managers after which they let the money flow in. Well; you will find that it doesn't work like that.

Yes, you will sit back and wait for the money to come in, but you still have to be active to some extent to make the dream of passive income true.

To achieve passive income, you need to follow a few tips:

1. *Focus on profitable assets.* To build a passive income from your real estate properties, you need to have enough capital in the first place. After this, you need to invest in properties that will give you returns that are enough for you to sit back and delegate the tasks.
2. *Start as soon as possible.* Passive income cannot just start the next day–it takes ages for you to realize this income. Gone are the days when you could make profits in such a short time. Now, you have to build your business for several years before you hit the jackpot.
3. *Know how much passive income you need.* As important as you desire to have passive income, you need to have a goal; it can be anything from saving to buy another property to generating enough income to pay for your basic expenses.
4. *Delegation in real estate investing.* Many investors have a hard time letting go of their jobs despite having experts that can handle the various tasks. Most of them approach their business as a 9-5 job. It is a fact that running a real estate business is not as easy as you might think, because you have many tasks that you need to handle.

You have to wake up and fulfill the appointments that you have as well as leads. You also have to complete a lot of paperwork before the day ends. These take a lot of time, and with the time you find that you have a lot of backlogs, giving you little time to focus on the business. You need to get some help.

You need to get someone to assist you with the tasks — not just any help, but professional help. You have to delegate some aspects of the business to these experts. The tasks that you delegate include updating listings, managing the marketing, and searching for new leads.

Without the right help, you are looking at poor management of clients— lose of deals and bad marketing, which cost you much in your business. Delegating tasks will help you boost revenue and give you time to focus on other profitable tasks.

Many people can help you to perform the tasks, but only a few will be able to do the work that you need them to do efficiently. Real estate markets are a specialist industry that needs experts in the area to handle the tasks. Having the right assistant makes things easy because they also give you access to the best deals and information.

The experts you work with should be professionals and be able to stick to a schedule and be there when you need them to be. This is ideal so that when you delegate any tasks to them, you are sure that it will be done before a deadline.

What to Delegate Based on Experience

The way you delegate depends on how far up the business you have gone. Let us look at the various aspects you can delegate under each category.

- *Newbie:* As a newbie, you don't have the experience to handle some tasks. Look for a professional that will have all the expertise you need. However, make sure you run most of the tasks by yourself so that you gain the experience you need and become better at trading.

Handling outsources is not a simple task; it needs a lot of time and effort. As you gain experience, you can outsource smaller tasks such as data entry. You also need to delegate repairs to experts.

- *Mid-Level Investor:* Here, you have some experience in the market, and you have many transactions in the market. You can outsource property management, marketing, handling the paperwork.
- *Top-Level Investor:* Apart from the tasks that have been mentioned above, you also need to outsource the various operations to the expert. You can even outsource the activities that involve sales.

Are You Ready to Invest Yet?

You need to know that real estate isn't just a business investment, but it is a commitment that you need to do as well. This is because if you decide to take up the responsibility of running investment properties, you need to be prepared as well.

Investing in real estate doesn't stop when you pay for a property — it goes way beyond this. You will face a lot of costs, refurbishment requests, taxes, and upkeep. If these costs are way more than what you are making in real estate, then you will find it hard disposing of the property.

So, don't believe the ads on television telling you that anyone can make a killing with real estate because it is not a guarantee.

So, how do you know you are ready for the big plunge into the real estate market? Here are a few pointers:

- *Your finances are in good order.* To know if you are ready to handle the costs that come with real estate investments, you need to check your spending. You need to have enough savings because of the properties that you plan to invest in need a lot of money. Since you will have to depend partly on loans, it is prudent that you improve your credit score. With a good credit score, you can apply and get approved for loans that you use to invest in properties.

- *You are ready to learn.* Being an investor isn't as simple as you renting out your house to a client and then thinking that you have all it takes to be termed an investor—it encompasses more. First, you need to understand that each county or state has its own rules that define the rights of the tenant as well as that of the investor. In some states, you need to have a security deposit, which is different from the owner's funds. Tenants that don't follow this rule end up with penalties.
- *You know your market.* When you decide to go into the real estate market, you need to make sure you know what you are planning to do. Identify the area and then go ahead to find as much information about the area as possible. Know about how the market behaves, why it behaves so, and the potential of closing deals the right way.
- *You know your abilities.* What are you good at when it comes to running real estate deals? Can you negotiate a better purchase price for better returns or can you spot goldmines in terms of buildings for flipping? Either way, your capabilities need to achieve your goals.

- *You can handle tenant needs.* The tenant is king always. When a property that you purchase sits empty, you lose money on the investment. This is why it is vital that you make sure you know how to handle repairs and vacancies. One of the biggest reasons why many landlords lose tenants is because of mistakes made by landlords.
- *You have financial goals.* Another sign that you are ready to start is you have clear financial goals that you go after. This can be saving up money for a new car or retirement—these are goals that make you invest in real estate. Before you take out a loan to start your business, you need to work closely with a mortgage lender on how the debt will affect your current situation.

Knowledge is Power When It Comes to Real Estate Investment

Investing in real estate is a sum of careful planning and knowing what to do and when to do it. Learning how to invest needs you to understand the market as well as the investments that are available for you to explore.

Let us look at the various resources that give you the knowledge you need so that you make factual decisions.

- *Books:* These give you insights into various real estate investment aspects. When you have the right book, you decide when to read and what to read without a lot of distractions. You can get a good book at just a few dollars, or you can opt for the free ones that are available in libraries. Choose a book that has been written by an investor with proven experience. It is best for the investor to have relevant experience in the sector which you have passion for. If possible, the book ought to give you project samples so that you have a clear understanding of what you are reading.
- *Online Resources:* With the advent of technology, training has become easy and accessible. With online resources, you can learn on-the-go, and it is more convenient compared to other traditional learning methods. You have hundreds of resources to choose from, with each approach giving you a style that suits your needs. There are available trainings the whole day and night. You can learn at your own pace, and lessons can be anything between a few minutes to a few hours each day. You can also start and stop anytime you feel like and resume from where you left it off.
- *Seminars:* These are offered in person or online via various platforms. The seminars can take the whole day or just a few hours. The best thing about seminars

is that you can access the videos then review any content that you missed out on.
- *Expert Mentoring:* This is the best method to learn real estate investment. An expert gives you one-on-one guidance using content that he has gained over the years. The person that mentors you might be someone that you already know or one that is interested in sharing the knowledge he has accumulated over the years.

Using an expert is ideal because you get the best hands-on learning while you work through a variety of practical items. These experts can also advise you when you hit a barrier, unlike in a book.

You can also get mentorship by reading stories that have been written by these industry leaders.

Investing isn't all about the process of buying and selling real estate; you also need to know how to delegate as discussed earlier. To know more about delegating, you need to read leadership books.

- *Keep a Journal:* As for other businesses, you need to make sure that you keep information on your dealings. This information will serve as a reference for the actions that you take. Many people ignore this step but find out later on that they need information, yet they don't have a source. Some of the information that you need to note down are the dates of different transactions, the goals of each, as well as details of each sale. You can start writing the information in brief then expand on them to include details.

Chapter : 3
Real Estate Investment Mistakes

Real estate investing is hard. You have to meet a lot of challenges that you never expected in the first place. But after you overcome these challenges, you enjoy enormous benefits.

In real estate investing, there are various barriers to entry; but the good thing is that the barriers also keep out the competition that is just looking for an easy ride. As time goes by, it becomes much easier to overcome these barriers to entry.

The aim is to test whether you have the necessary willpower to hold on and make it through. Will you stick to the plan or will you give up due to the challenges.

The challenges might last months, even years, but with the right strategy and with proper knowledge, you can become one of the best investors — you have to keep at it.

Unfortunately, real estate investing doesn't just have a single barrier to entry but several of them. Let us look at a few of these barriers.

- *Large initial capital outlay.* This is probably the biggest barrier to newbies trying to get into the real estate market. Real estate needs you to have more capital than any other type of investment, and many investors can't generate the capital needed. Remember that at least a 20 percent down payment is needed to start investing.

- *It is hard to find good deals.* The hardest part of real estate investing is finding the best deals to invest in. A look at the market will reveal that most of the available deals don't necessarily give you a great investment. The parts of real estate that purport to have the best deals are congested with investors, making competition too fierce.

This barrier is a bigger challenge for new investors, just getting into the market. You will find that it takes you a long time to get the first deal to invest in. The reason behind this is that you have a lot to learn and you are new to a lot of the things that happen in real estate investing.

While at it, you will learn that for you to find the best prospects. You have to look at so many leads to get the prospects that will turn into a great deal.

So, you need to be ready to learn a lot and be patient as you hunt for the best deals that will catapult your career in the right direction.

- *Lacking the requirements to qualify for a bank loan.* Many investors didn't start with their investments; instead, they had to apply for and qualify for bank loans. As a new investor, you need to apply for a loan to cover for the 20% of the cost of the property. While you have a wide selection of finance options that you can choose from, the requirements can end up being overwhelming. First, your credit score has to top because this will give you better interest rates as well.
- *Repair isn't as easy as you think.* Many investors watch remodel TV shows and believe that it is easy to buy a house, remodel it, and then flip it for profit. The truth is that it isn't as easy as you think. Once you know this, you will still face some challenges that will scare away, even the best buyers.

After going past these barriers, many investors think that they now have the right to make money in real estate investing, and they relax. They don't know that this is now the time to ramp it up and work harder to make money in real estate.

Mistakes in real estate investing are normal, and while these mistakes are all too common, you need to find a way to handle them. Traders, whether new to the game or experienced traders, make mistakes time and again. The only thing that differentiates winners from losers is that winning investors know what to do to mitigate the mistakes.

Let us look at the common mistakes that many people do in real estate investing and what to do to mitigate them.

1. *Failure to Research.* Research forms the ultimate basis for entry into the market. When you plan to start investing in real estate, you have to make a lot of decisions. These decisions are the ones that will determine the success of your strategy.

It is just prudent that before you invest in real estate, you need to compare different properties, ask as many questions as you can and determine whether the property you want to purchase is worth the money you will pay. This due diligence serves to give you the right direction towards fulfilling your investment goals.

Before you can come up with a conclusion, you have to also ask specific questions regarding each type of property category. For instance, the research you undertake for buy-and-hold properties isn't the same type of research that you will undertake for a property that you plan to fix and flip.

Not only do you have to ask many questions regarding the home, but you also need to ask about the neighborhood where the property is situated. Here are a few questions that shouldn't miss on a potential property investor checklist:

- Does the property have access to basic services and facilities?
- What is the average price for homes in the area?
- Does the home have any licensing issues that need to be handled before the purchase?
- Does the home need anything to be replaced, such as fixtures and other installations? How much will the whole process cost?
- What are the reasons that make the owner sell the house?

Answering these and many other questions make it possible for you to get the perfect property to invest in.

2. *Going for Lousy Finance Option.* The real aim of having finance options is to try and give you get properties that you would otherwise not afford using your savings. The downside is that many investors are always in a hurry, and they end up working with lenders who don't have their interest at heart. Once you have the financing in place is when you realize that the interest rates aren't as friendly as you thought. Here, the main point we are emphasizing is that you need to

have the financial flexibility to pay back the loan even if you are asked to pay more in terms of interest.

3. *Running the Business on Your Own.* It is a fact that many investors enter the market and decide to do everything on their own just because they don't trust anyone. Many of the investors believe that they know everything there is to know about real estate investing and that they can go ahead and close deals on their own without any help from experts.

The truth is that even if you have closed many deals before, the process doesn't always go as smoothly as it always goes. When things go south, you need to have someone you can turn to to fix the issue. This is when you need to have an expert to work with.

We have talked about delegation in the previous chapters, but at times you also have to consult with professionals so that you understand what you need to do at that time.

You need to make sure you have a list of experts in the area you work with because having to seek help far from where the business is located translates into more costs for you.

The list of experts should include a handyman, real estate agent, home inspector, insurance representative, and a competent attorney. These ought to be able to tell you about any property you plan to buy even before you commit to purchase it. They will be able to advise you on what to do and what not to do.

In the case of the attorney, he advises you on the issues regarding the title or licenses that might come to haunt you down the line.

4. *Paying More than You Ought To.* When you perform the right research, you will end up with a property that gives you all the benefits that you dream of–easy to sell and a handsome profit. However, the reverse is also true–lack of enough research translates into a flopped sell or purchase.

Finding the right property can be slow and frustrating. When you finally get that property that meets your needs and wants as an investor, the seller might fail to accept your bid for the property.

Lack of research is usually a result of anxiety in the investor. For instance, you plan to buy a property, and you feel that when you don't get it, you might not make money this month. This pushes you to make rash decisions that might not go down well with your strategy.

Since the house might have attracted various bidders, you decide to overbid so that you win the bid. Overbidding has many negative consequences, top on the list being debt. When you overbid on a house you end up borrowing money to cover for the deficit-you end up in debt. It might take you several years before you can make returns on your investment.

To know whether the investment you are chasing is within your price range or way above the right price, you need to start looking at other similar homes and what has been paid for them over the past recent months. You can get this information from a real estate broker from the area. If you cannot get this information from a broker, then you need to compare similar homes that have been listed in the local directory and see if you can find a similar home. Unless the home offers better features that are likely to make it more attractive to buyers, then you need to stick to the price range as per other homes in the area.

You need to keep in mind that there are also other opportunities in the area that you can take up if the current one doesn't go through. You can always get another property that will meet your needs; all you need to do is to be patient when performing the search.

5. *Underestimating the Costs.* Investors can agree that owning a property isn't all about paying for it, and that is all-there are a lot of expenses that you will have to pay. These include maintenance costs as well as other

costs that are associated with furnishing the house, repairs, and many more. Property taxes, as well as insurance costs, are a huge part of the expenses in a property.

The major mistake that new investors make in this regard is forgetting costs that are associated with searching for a property to flip or hold onto.

The solution to this is to come up with a list of all the costs that come up when you buy and run a property, whether rental or for flipping. Once you add up all the expenses, you get the right idea whether you will make money out of the deal or it will be a cash drain. Once you add the numbers, you will have a good idea of the costs that are associated with the property and whether you can afford it. Additionally, you know if you have a chance of making a profit out of the property.

The practice of numbers is more important to investors and flippers. This is all because profits are usually linked to the selling price minus the different costs of buying and sprucing up the property.

Some of the costs that you need to look at include cancellation fees and more.

6   *Not Picking the Right Location.* As an investor, the location of the property is a key concept. Location

forms the main factor for the success or failure of your investment. Many buyers look at the location because it determines many factors that will impact on the happiness, comfort, and safety of the family. Purchasing a property in the wrong location can be a costly mistake.

As an investor, you need to look at various aspects of the location to make everything work out for you:

- *Quality of the neighborhood:* consider the neatness of the area or whether it is full of debris. What is the condition of the compound? After the analysis, you need to come back with a snapshot of the area that tells you all about the neighborhood, street, and the community that surrounds the property.
- *Amenities:* look at the factors that determine access to transport, healthcare, and ecommerce. After you have a list of the various items, rank them according to importance. This way, you have a rough idea what kind of clientele the area will serve.
- *Access to the transport network*: many clients don't want to spend a lot to access transport networks in an area. They usually opt to stay close to roads so that they can travel to work in the shortest time possible.

- *Value of Property:* consider the popularity of the area. At times this popularity can extend to neighboring areas and affect the prices of various properties.
- *Schools:* many clients that have children are very concerned about the education of their children and will often pay more money for properties that are located in an area with learning institutions.
- *Security:* when it comes to security, you have no compromise at all. One thing you are sure of is that no one will be willing to live in an insecure community. Everyone wants to be safe in the confines of their homes and walk the streets at any time of day without getting mugged.

All these factors and many more others are important in choosing the ideal property for sale. However, not all investors know where to choose the right property and end up with a property that they can't sell off. Undesirable location feature decreases the value of the property and makes it hard to sell it off.

Additionally, the location dictates the cost of running the property. Remember that taxes you pay vary from one property to another and from one location to another as well.

7 *Not Choosing the Right Property for Your Strategy.* After you have completed research and decided on which

property to invest in, the next step is to pick the right property that you can invest in and make a profit out of it.

Many new investors fail at this step, and they end up making a lot of losses, only to learn from their mistakes later on.

One of the top mistakes that investors make when choosing a property to put their money in is falling in love with a property. Emotions run high when you are looking to buy a property, and many buyers end up looking for a property that appeals to them rather than for one that is ideal for their clients.

Make sure you eliminate the aspect of emotions when looking for the perfect property to sell or hold on.

Another mistake that buyers make is to make hasty decisions. When this happens, you need to look at various properties in an area before you make the final decision. With the properties in file, talk to property consultants and see what they say about the capability of all the properties you have on file. With various options to consider, you can get the right one at a good price.

When choosing the right property, make sure you look at how much it costs to maintain it. Remember that you came into the business to make as much profit as possible from the after sale profit or from rental income, while reducing on the expenses that come with maintaining the property. This is why it is ideal for getting a property inspector to inspect the property before you go ahead with the purchase.

You also need to find out how much rental income to expect. Do this by finding out how much other properties in the area are being paid for in terms of rent.

Failure to get the right property makes it hard for you to get the right returns when you close the deal.

8 *Failure to Choose the Right Strategy.* One of the most important aspects of successful real estate investment is having the right strategy. Choosing a poor strategy is just that – you end up failing miserably. For example, if you have a short time to invest, it is not ideal to go for a buy and hold.

So, make sure you choose the right strategy depending on your capability, available time, and your finances.

Other factors that affect the strategy include the expectations, changes in demand, as well as inflation.

Not having a strategy is a huge mistake for every trader. Every great investor has a strategy that they follow to the latter, and they have studied the strategy in detail so that they nail the process every time. The more defined your strategy is, the less time you will lose when entering a trade and the fewer mistakes you will make.

9. *Miscalculating the Budget.* As an investor, you need to run numbers regularly, whether you are calculating the cost of repairs or taxes. Let us look at the common mistakes that arise when you run a budget, and how you can eliminate them.

Failure to budget for unexpected repairs makes it hard for you to know what you will enjoy in the form of profits. At times you will be lucky not to get a property that needs repairs, but when you go for long term investments, you must include repairs in your budget. The same can be said for projects that take longer than you expected. For instance, a project that was to take a few weeks can take one more month to complete, which translates into extra costs.

Locking out property management has caught many investors on the wrong footing. You might decide to manage the property by yourself, but when you start receiving calls as late as 3 am from tenants, you then understand the need for a property manager. The truth is that at one time or another, you will have to call in the services of a property manager.

Failure to budget for these and many other costs ends up frustrating you later on when you realize that the amount you expected as profit isn't real. Make sure you understand all the costs that are related to the property and make sure you estimate the costs the right way.

> 10 *Starting Too Late.* Many investors have this notion that starting in real estate is only possible when you have the right amount of cash. They also insist that to make money in real estate; you need to have all the money you need in full. This isn't true because there are various financing options that you can take advantage of.

Remember that real estate investing is a task that you learn through practice; therefore, it is always better to start early than later. Additionally, the earlier you start, the better because making money in real estate takes time and patience.

> 11 *Starting Too Big Too Soon.* When you start investing in real estate, you find that you have the chance to start at whatever level you desire. Some people start small while others start big. For most of them, desire to get rich too quickly makes them go for plans that are too big for them.

You need to understand, as discussed earlier, this business needs you to be patient and work harder than ever before. You also need to understand that this plan only works when you learn the trade from other experts in the real estate investment market.

When you are starting, don't overwhelm yourself with a level that you cannot handle otherwise you might go bankrupt so fast. For your safety, start small and then use the opportunity to grow the business.

12. *Going for an Expert When You Can't Afford It.* As an investor, you need to only go for a service that you can afford. Remember, your main aim is to make sure you make some profits as an investor. When it comes to getting a manager for your property, you need to make sure you have enough funds to sustain the venture. For many people, they think that they need to have experts whatever the costs, only to discover that they aren't making any profits from the sale of property due to heightened expenses.
13. *Not Getting Expert Advice When You Can Afford it.* In the same vein, if you are investing and you have more profitable tasks to do than paint walls and renovate your property, you need to have a property manager to handle these tasks for you. The manager saves you a lot

of time and energy that you can devote to other aspects of the business.

14 *Failure to Learn from Mistakes.* This might be the worst of all mistakes that you can make as a real estate investor. You will make a lot of mistakes, but you need to find a way to learn from these mistakes. Learning from your mistakes is when you find a way to do things better the next time. After every issue, you need to draw up the right conclusions then learn the right lessons so that you don't repeat them in subsequent trades.

Chapter : 4
Real Estate Investment Strategies

Real estate comes with a lot of opportunities that you can take advantage of as an investor. The opportunities differ in terms of what you need to invest, the work involved, and the profits you enjoy.

As an investor, you will have a wide choice to pick from that will make you profit. Let us look at the different opportunities and what you need to do as an investor.

Rental Properties

As an investor, you buy a rental property to earn income from it. Rental properties can range from single family homes to multiple family homes. They can be commercial properties that rent out office space to businesses. You make money from the rent that you collect each month.

You work on leases, which can be short term (less than 3 years) or long term (more than 3 years).

Here are the top reasons why you might consider rental property as an investment:

1. *You are in control.* When you go down rental property lane, you have full control of your property. It is all for you to choose the kind and size of property to invest on, decide who to rent out the property to, and how much each tenant will pay and when. You also decide how you manage your property.

When you are working in a 9-5 job, you are at the full whims of the boss. You do what the boss needs at whatever time he needs you to do it. Investing in stocks can give you some freedom as well, but still, you are under a little control, especially when it comes to choosing in the security to trade in.

With rental properties, things are different: you do what you want when you want it, as long as it is in line with your goals.

2. *Appreciation of property.* A unique thing about being a real estate investor is that once you buy it, the value increases after a few years down the line. This gives you profit, especially if you choose to buy the property using your savings.

Additionally, when you take out a loan to buy the property, the rent income helps you to clear the loan over the years. You don't have to rely entirely on your savings to do this.

When you decide to sell the property off, you get more leverage because of the appreciation that has come up with the property for all the years.

3. *You enjoy income from the property.* When you rent out the property to tenants, you get an income after every period. Using the money, you can pay off any expenses after which you are left with money in the pocket.

For instance, you have ten tenants that pay $1,000 per month and your expenses total to $7,000 per month; you end up with $3,000 that you can use for whatever task you wish.

4. *Tax deductions.* As an owner of rental property, you are assured of tax deductions from the government. You get to write off various taxes such as mortgage interest, insurance, maintenance repairs, and many more. Besides, you can depreciate the cost of your property based on a preset schedule, regardless of the appreciation of the property.

As much as you are enjoying the advantages of owning a rental property, you also face various disadvantages. These include:

1. *Tenant risk.* You don't have a definite guarantee that the tenants will pay their rent on time. Some tenants pay religiously, while other tenants won't pay the rent at

all. Eviction takes time and money, which means you need to screen your tenants before you decide to allow them to take up the houses.

If you take the whole issue personally, you might end up without tenants in your property, which translates into a lack of income for you each month.

Some tenants are careless and lead to wear off your property compared to others. Well, you might have the security deposit, but remember that some damages cost more than what the tenant paid as a deposit.

2. *It takes a big chunk out of your capital.* One of the demerits of investing in rental property is that you have to pay a lot to achieve the dream. Putting a lot of funds in a single investment leads to a concentration of assets, which beats diversifications. If the neighborhood deteriorates, you will lose a lot of money. However, if you have a lot of wealth, this isn't such a huge factor at all.

3. *High property taxes.* Every state has a certain amount that you pay as property tax. You have to pay this tax regardless of whether the houses are occupied or not. The cost is usually steady and is usually communicated to you in advance. The bottom line is that this cost usually cuts right into your profits, and it is so painful,

especially when you don't have someone renting the property.

4. *Requires your active involvement.* You might decide to delegate the running of the rental property to the property manager, which is a good thing to do, but you still have to put in some time to make sure everything works well. Additionally, when you hire a property management company, you reduce the profit margin that you would have received.

Flipping Houses

Finding success in real estate is more than just buying a rental property then looking for tenants to enjoy the rent—you can also choose to buy a property, renovate it, then flip it.

What is flipping in the first place? When we talk about house flipping, we are looking at the process of buying a property that is foreclosed or distressed with the intention of renovating it and selling it off at a profit within a short period.

If you are planning to make use of this aspect of investing, you need to come up with the right strategy, and then execute the best plan.

Before you can jump into the house flipping business, you need to acquire enough knowledge about the industry so that you don't make the mistakes that many new investors make.

First, know your skill level depending on the experience you have. For instance, make sure you understand to what extent you can handle renovations that you will oversee.

Additionally, make sure you understand the market you are going to be part of. Talk to pro investors and local homeowners so that you know more about the market.

After understanding these two, you need to understand the applicable taxes and other rules that touch on real estate. When this is done, it is now time to understand how much money you have for the task at hand. Knowing the amount of money you can set aside for the business makes sure you come up with the best budget and identifying the losses that come with house flipping.

The Process of Flipping Houses

When it comes to flipping houses, you need to meet a few requirements that include:

- *Have a business plan.* Before you make any move, you need to write a business plan. The business plan helps you determine the scope of your investments, placing caps and limits on the investments, show the budgeting plans as well as determine the decisions about the type of real estate.

- *Start with what you know.* You need to know what you have at the moment so that you can take maximum advantage of the strengths that you possess. The assets you can take advantage of include networks of investors and more.

Talk to colleagues, friends, and relatives that are in the business or that have experience working in the sector. These sources can help you find reputable contractors, wholesalers, and even buyers.

Once you have the team, you need to reach out to the network to give you contacts in the industry, and then seek out these experts for advice. You can also join local investment groups so that you connect with like-minded people.

- *Come up with a team.* You need to have a qualified team on board so that you don't do everything by yourself. When coming up with the right team, look at the various roles that you plan to outsource, and then assign each role to a professional before you contact them.

Barriers to Flipping Houses

The process of flipping houses for profit isn't as easy as you might think. Here are some of the challenges you will encounter in your journey to flip houses the right way:

- *Getting the right deals.* When you are starting, you might think that getting the property to flip is easy, but it isn't. With many traders looking for the best houses to flip, good deals rarely come by. This becomes hard, especially for new investors who don't have enough capital to put down.
- *Acquiring finance.* When flipping houses, you have to pay for many issues that affect the property, including paying for repairs. You can choose to look for finance for flipping the property but even getting this money isn't easy at all.
- *Property repair.* To flip a house, you need to make sure you get the right contractor to do the flips. Without quality, you are looking at a loss in term of failure to get someone to buy the house. Poor workmanship might end up costing you more than you ever thought of. Additionally, you have to work with affordable contractors so that you realize your profit margin.
- *Making a profit.* This is another challenge that most investors face when flipping houses. Every repair

needs to be cost-effective so that you get something out of what you put in.

Sources of Finance When Flipping Houses

When it comes to flipping houses, you have a variety of sources that you can use to get the money to put up. Here are the various options you have to find the finance for your task.

- *Savings:* Here, you depend solely on your savings. For this to work, you need to have enough cash saved up for it to be meaningful. You have to use your savings to pay for the property, repair as well as all the costs.
- *Bank Finance:* Many banks don't lend money to flippers, though some banks will do on strict repayment terms. Every bank has a different program for flippers, so it is best that you interact with the bank to know where they stand when it comes to lending.
- *Private Money:* This is money that you source from family, friends, and other people that are close to you. You can approach a family member and come up with terms that you will pay back the money later. However, even though they are part of your family, they will take time before you can get money from them. You have to prove that you are trustworthy and you can deliver the business before you get the money.

- *Hard Money Lenders:* These were meant to lend money to investors looking for hard cash for funding their exploits. However,
- *Partners:* Working with a partner can be such a great way to begin when you don't have enough funds to invest.

The Pros and Cons of Property Flipping

You need to know the advantage and disadvantages of flipping properties before you can start the process. Every real estate business has its risks, but when it comes to the flipping property, this becomes riskier. You can end up with great rewards if you do thing s the way they need to be done, and everything moves according to plan. However, it can become a terrible mistake when you don't follow the plan as expected.

The Pros of Flipping Property

- *Quick profit:* This is the main reason many people enter the business—to make money fast. If you do this correctly, the business can give you a lot of profits. You can achieve the high returns in such a short period that you will be surprised. For many investors, this takes only a few months.
- *Gain necessary experience:* When you flip properties several times a year, you get adept at the business, and

soon you will understand various aspects of flipping such as construction, rehabilitation, renovation, and many more. From the various practices, you understand the various costs of material as well as electrical installations. The experience you gain gives you a lot of leverage for many future projects.

- *Gives you vital buyer insights*: Once you place a few properties on the market successfully, you gain proper insight into what the buyers in the market want from investors. This allows you to come up with the right adjustments to properties before you put them up for sale.
- *Understand budgeting:* Budgeting is one of the enormous challenges that investors encounter, especially when you have a lot of unanticipated costs coming up.
- *Grow your contacts:* When you start flipping property, you get to rub shoulders with who is who in the market such as attorneys, realtors, inspectors, brokers, and other parties. These contacts are vital for future investments in such a way that you can consult with them whenever you feel like.

The Cons of Flipping Properties

The business has advantages, but it also comes with various disadvantages that you need to be aware of when you attempt to get into the market.

- *Losses:* The major problem with flipping a property for profit is that you lose money when the flip goes south. Various factors contribute to this loss, including unanticipated costs, high taxes, and the costs of holding onto the property.
- *Difficulty in selling the property:* If you can't find a buyer for the property, you will end up with difficulty in selling the property. Holding onto the property means you have to pay various expenses. The longer you hold onto the property, the more you lose in terms of costs. Additionally, when the property sits on the market for too long, you end up selling it at a loss.

These pros and cons let you know whether to take up the property or not.

Wholesaling Real Estate

Wholesaling houses is an easy task to do, but it isn't as easy as it seems.

Many investors aren't privy over the details of wholesaling, but the concept is simple: you buy and sell houses without renovating it or doing any repairs. You might also acquire a house on contract then sign off the contract to someone else.

For the investors who know how it operates, they start with wholesaling because they know it isn't as capital intensive as other methods.

The aim is to get a house that is on sale and then sell it off at a profit. The wholesaler sells the house off to investors who can pay in cash. The houses don't require any financing or appraisals because there is no time to do this.

Wholesalers don't need to own any money of their own because they use a double contract. When you go for a double contract, you use the money that you get from the buyer to pay the seller, taking your cut during the transaction.

How Does the Deal Work?

The process of finding houses on wholesale terms is a bit complicated, that is if you don't know what you are doing. On the contrary, if you know what you need and how to do everything, you get the capacity to handle the deal fast. Here is the process:

1. *Identify the deal:* You need to identify a property that is up for sale, and it fits the bill for wholesaling. For one, you can locate a property that has absentee owners and sends them postcards to see if they are interested in selling the property to you. Absentee owners are the best to work with because they don't live so much in the house and might have tenants that aren't good at all.
2. *Understand the underlying contract:* When you identify a potential deal, the next step is for you to talk to the person in charge of the property and acquire it under contract. You need to know the various details of the house and what the investor is offering. You ought to be sure that you can get the property under contract for an amount that is less than what the investor will pay. Remember, you aim to make a profit from the contract price and what the buyer pays.
3. *Get the buyer:* Once you have acquired the house under contract, it is now time to make sure you get the right buyer for the property. The buyer needs to be ready to pay a price that will give you a profit. Depending on the agreement, you need to request the investor to submit a deposit (non-refundable) with a title company of their choice. This is for the fact that when the investor refuses to sign the contract at the end of it all, you get something out of your efforts.

4. *Close the deal:* Once the property has been deemed fit for the deal at hand, the title company sets up the closing with all the paperwork and have a schedule for the day for signing the papers.

As a wholesaler, your role is to make sure that the property remains in the same condition as described and that it is vacant and accessible to the investor.

Mistakes that Wholesalers Make

Many wholesalers need up with a flopped deal because of a few mistakes that they make during the deal. Let us check out a few mistakes that make it hard for the wholesaler to make a profit from deals.

- *Not knowing what an investor plans to pay:* Going into a wholesale deal, blindly makes it hard for you to understand how much money you will make on the deal. Many wholesalers think that just because they have found a deal that looks lucrative, they will make money out of it. For your information, if you don't find a deal that is cheap enough for you to sell it off and make a profit, then none of the buyers will go for the deal no matter the number of buyers you have listed down.

- *Creating numbers from rumors:* Many wholesalers come up with numbers because they don't know the real numbers. Most of these don't have the time to do research when making purchases, which means they base on guesswork when coming up with numbers. Other wholesalers don't have the time to create the perfect budget. They leave out many costs, such as closing costs, selling costs, and many others. When the deal isn't as specific as it needs to be, the investor ends up losing money on the deal, and you end up looking like a fool just because you didn't have the right information to post.

Benefits of Wholesaling Real Estate

As much as it is complicated, this style of investing comes with several benefits that you need to know before you go into the business.

- *Ideal for beginners:* This form of investing is easier to start than other strategies. The process doesn't require extensive licensing or knowledge about remodeling properties. The expenses are also less compared to other investment options making it the best for beginners.

- *Easy to learn:* The right knowledge can turn any basics into profit. There is enough information out there to give you more than what you need in terms of guidance. You can run your wholesale tasks hands-on so that you learn from the many mistakes that you will make.
- *Fast cash:* Wholesaling gives you the opportunity of getting paid faster than ever. Compared to holding onto land or coming up with new construction, which takes years to pay off, you are looking at high returns after a few days or hours.
- *No need to consider location:* This mode of trading allows you to deal with properties from anywhere around the world. Al you need is to get the seller to sign the contract and a buyer to close the deal.
- *No finance required:* Even with bad credit, you can still enjoy the profits from wholesaling trades. The process is such that you don't have to buy property; all you have to do is to sign a contract and transfer it to another person. Your role is just to form a connection between the seller and the buyer.
- *Gain valuable experience:* Wholesaling in real estate is one of the best ways to get the necessary experience to immerse yourself deeper in the industry. From the knowledge you acquire, you get to understand the basics as well as the advances in property trading.

Disadvantages of Wholesaling Real Estate

Wholesaling real estate also comes with a few cons that you need to understand.

- *No guaranteed income:* Sadly, this strategy doesn't give you a guaranteed income every day – it is not like a 9-5 job whereby you will have a paycheck every end month. You don't have retirement benefits and insurance for wholesaling properties. If you plan to make it a full-time job, you need to be that person who can manage your finances well.
- *Failure to find a buyer:* As a successful wholesaler, you need to have a list of buyers before you can start placing the property on the market. Without a buyer, you have no deal to follow through. Remember that the buyer will require you to pay him if you waste his time without anything concrete for him to see.

So, before you think of selling property, you need to have a list of potential buyers who are lined up for the property before you make an offer to the seller.

Automatic Entrances Make Life Easier for You

When selling off properties, you need to make sure that there is a selling point that appeals to the buyer so that you sell it off faster. One of the top features that new homeowners are looking for is the automatic entrance.

If you desire to sell your property faster, then having an automatic entrance is a plus for you. This, in addition to other features, places you in pole position to close the deal the best way you can.

Delegation is Still Vital

When deciding on which type of investment you wish to take part in, you need to have a team that will help you come up with deals and close them. Take time to understand what roles each player in the team will handle and find the various experts to handle these roles.

When entering a trade, you need to ask yourself, "How can I earn more, working less?"

Chapter : 5
Leverage in Real Estate Investments

Have you ever looked at a real estate investor and wondered what goes on in their thoughts? Have you ever asked yourself what they think and what pushes them to succeed?

Everyone desires success, but chasing it takes a long and arduous process that isn't easy for many people. The good thing is that you have people to guide you.

You can spend thousands of dollars paying for videos, books, and much more documentation, but at the end of the day, there are a few principles that these documents cannot give you — the secret recipe for success that every Investor worth his salt holds dear.

This chapter explores the mindset of a successful real estate investor and attempts to get you into their heads so that you can know what to do when the time comes to make those tough decisions.

The Mindset of the Successful Real Estate Investor

1. *Never to dwell on mistakes.* Mistakes happen, just like any other business out there. And when they happen, there are those investors that sit down and cry over spilled milk while there are those that take the next road to success.

They happen so that they can tell you what you did wrong where you need to learn the lessons intended to be learned and then move on.

When you fear mistakes, you end up hurting any prospects because of the inherent fear you have of messing up again. You won't examine the prospects with a clear mind.

So, what you need to do is to learn the lessons from your mistakes, then look at what happened and then move on to another deal.

2. *Don't compare; it makes everything hard on you.* Have you ever tried to make a deal only to look at what every person is doing then start loathing yourself, your methods? You might have heard of another investor that is doing better than you or they grabbed a deal that you have been after the whole time. You might realize that one of the new "kids on the block" has just bought

a new car from his proceeds and you wonder how that happened when you are struggling to make the first deal.

When you think about all of this, you try to convince yourself that investing isn't your forte. Well, you need to think twice before you start comparing your plans and strategies to another person's.

As an investor, the aspect of comparison sucks all the joy out of investing. You will gain a lot if you learn from what other people have gone through, but you will find that there's no single merit when you start comparing them. Doing this places you in the middle of the biggest pity party.

3. *Not everything is controllable.* Every trader tries to have as much control as possible over the trades they place, but this isn't the way it sounds. You need to accept that there are some situations you can control and some you can't. Some situations will get out of hand so fast that you will wonder what happened in the first place.
4. *Worrying isn't part of the plan.* Many people worry not because something is going wrong, but just because they haven't met the target yet. As a trader, the right mindset is not to worry about the trader or potential issues — it makes you work out. Successful real estate

investors don't have the time to worry, especially about future deals—they just handle the issue when it arises.

5. *Workaholism isn't part of the deal.* New traders will seek to work day and night looking for that winning deal that will change their life. They feel that when they stop, everything will stop. If you are a trader that is serious about what you do, you embrace delegation so that you give some roles to experts.

Successful traders take some time off to rest because they understand that some of their best works are done when they are fresh and clear-headed. They know that making it in the market isn't all about working as hard as possible but smart.

6 *Advice is always welcome.* Any investor knows that it is vital to get a second opinion from experts in the market. They not only expect positive feedback but negative observations as well. Many new investors ignore any complaints as well. They sit, listen, and then investigate whatever they hear before they react to it. They understand that listening and making adjustments is the only way they can improve their strategies.

7 *They use facts.* Facts represent anything when it comes to making decisions. It all boils down to gathering the right information, analyzing the information at hand, and then deciding the information that has been

collected. This means that the information is based on facts, not just hearsay, and rumors.

8 *Only the best gets the nod.* Every successful investor that you will come across will tell you one thing: always provide the best service and you will see more clients come in. These investors are proud of the work they do and give the client the best property ever. They don't take any corner when looking for that property — they go the whole nine yards.

They make sure they start with high standards, and then they maintain it. They also make sure their clients also maintain these standards in anything they do.

A successful investor isn't only after that quick buck, but o try and have repeat customers.

9 *Patience pays.* This trait might sound so simple, but this isn't always the case. Real estate investing comes with a lot of pressure for you to close deals as fast as possible, but this isn't always what you need to do.

For many investors, the pressures are all about doing more, faster, and at a lower price compared to what they did before. It is also about making that profit.

Top investors understand that the pressure doesn't add any value to their goals. They understand that even though they need to move fast, still they need to pause and see how things are moving before making the next step. Patience isn't all about stopping to rest or wait for a deal to finalize; it might be as simple as identifying the areas that you aren't adept at and finding solutions that prevent you from making costly mistakes.

New investors are culprits of this trait; they come up with deadlines that dictate how they do their stuff. They put a lot of pressure on themselves to beat these deadlines that they forget that they need to review documents or change a certain aspect of the whole process.

Successful investors don't see the need to have a predetermined number of deals to close and will go ahead to do things step by step. They have the patience to sit and wait for the perfect deal to come through.

10 *Timing is everything.* A big problem for most new investors on the market is improper timing of deals. Many of them don't know when to jump into the market and end up going with the wave. Most of them feel that since everyone is buying properties, then this is the time to get involved. They don't have the strength to manage the friction that comes with investing.

Delegation

A real estate investor knows that he can't do everything alone and succeed. They understand the need to delegate some of the roles of an expert who can perform the roles entitled to them and help the process succeed.

With this in mind, let us look at the various experts that you can work with to make sure you achieve your goals as a real estate investor.

Real Estate Brokers

Running your real estate investment business is not as easy as you think; it involves a lot of tasks. One of the steps you should take to make life easier for you is to hire a real estate broker. The broker works on your behalf to get you the best deal on a property.

They help you get the property that you can trade in. So, as you can see, hiring a real estate broker is worth the money that you invest in.

Who Is a Broker?

As the name goes, this is a professional who has a license in brokerage to perform the following duties:

- Sells properties on your behalf.
- Understands the terms of any agreement as well as procedures.
- Determines the best price for your property so that you get a good deal.
- Works as an intermediary between you and your buyers, making sure you close a good deal on any property that you have on the market.
- Comes up with listings for your property so that your ads are active all the time.
- Assesses the value o property and makes sure they appraise the price as necessary.

How to Choose the Best Real Estate Broker

You realize that it is a tough task identifying and working with the right broker because the truth is that most of the good ones have been taken. The good news is that you can still get a few that are ready to work with you.

With so many to choose from, it becomes a challenge picking the right one. Here are a few pointers to what to look for when choosing the right broker for your investment:

- *Consider the services the broker provides.* When choosing a broker, it is vital that he provides the services that you need. Many investors focus so much on how much the broker charges that they forget that this isn't as vital as it seems.

Remember that if you get the right broker who provides the services you need at the best price, then you stand to gain more as compared to the end income. Additionally, you need to understand that you won't be with a brokerage forever, and it is allowed for you to change the broker to get the best services.

- *Look at the broker fees.* Most brokers will take 6 percent of the deal. This amount is split between the buyer's and sales agent. If you decide to hire a broker, it is vital that you look at the background of the broker and what he provides. Research the professional past of the broker, and if you find that he has a fine past, then it is worth taking up their services.
- *Availability.* Ideally, you hire someone that can be available when you need them. Some brokers won't be around to show the property when a client is on the scene. So, ask the real estate broker which times they work so that you know whether you have someone that takes their job seriously.
- *Find an expert in the area.* Find an expert that understands the area very well and knows a lot about the area. The agent also needs to be aware of the selling

prices and offerings than the other brokers in the area. To find such a broker, it is vital that you ask for referrals. You can also peruse the real estate publications to see which agents have a huge number of listings in the area.

- *Personality*. Investors need to look for agents that have a personality that blends with theirs. For you to sell a property quickly, you need to be on the same page with the broker. Both of you need to agree on when and how the home needs to be sold.

Advantages of Hiring a Real Estate Broker

So, why should you hire a real estate broker in the first place?

- *Enjoy local expertise*. If you plan to do business in a local area, you need to work with a local expert that understands everything there is about trading properties. Real estate brokers know what to do and have the knowledge to identify positive cash flow properties in a short time and manner at competitive prices. With the right rapport and communication, you can reap the benefits of working with a broker and having the right team on the ground.

Whether you plan to trade in single family homes or condos, the broker is much more qualified to guide you towards the right investment opportunities to enjoy returns for the long term.

- *Broker helps you keep up to date with market conditions.* The broker is better equipped to get the right investment property in a given area. These brokers have exclusive access to multiple listings; thus, they can get properties that you aren't knowledgeable about. The broker knows the best properties to give you top returns at any given time and conditions.
- *They guide you on how much* to pay or ask for a property. The brokers have a better sense of what the home is worth and are best equipped to give you competitive pricing of the property. If you are looking for information, they can streamline this process and make sure you get the information you seek in the shortest period. You are better of making a deal when you have an expert by your side opposed to doing things on your own.
- *Networking opportunities.* An experienced broker has the capacity of making negotiation and communication easy on your part. With the broker by your side, you are sure that you will get the maximum value on investment property, whether selling or buying the property. The broker acts as a mediator and helps you get the best deal for the real estate investment business.

- *Reduces the hassle of paperwork.* Just like any business, you have a lot of paperwork to handle whenever you get into an agreement. Real estate purchase or sale agreements aren't just 2-page contracts that you sign in a minute – most of them are lengthy documents with many clauses that you have to handle. If this is the first time you are looking to fulfill a trade, then you need to work with a broker that knows what to do so that you don't mess up.
- *Save a lot of time.* When you hire a broker, you take some of the tasks and transfer them to the broker. This reduces the need to learn everything there is about buying and selling properties so that you focus on core business functions.

However, this is only possible if you work with a broker who has the right knowledge to handle the tasks you delegate to him the right way. This is not only time-effective but also convenient for you.

- *Stay up to date with market trends.* Brokers have knowledge of and access to databases and analytical tools to understand and interpret market trends so that you can make better decisions regarding your investment property. This information is timely and handy for you as an investor.

Disadvantages of Working with a Broker

As much as it is advisable to work with a broker, it comes with a few demerits that you need to know.

- *High commission margins.* Working with a professional broker doesn't come cheaply, especially if the broker is highly qualified. You have to part with up to 6 percent of the cost of the house. This means that even if you don't make a profit from the sale of a property, you will have to pay the broker.
- *Time is an issue.* Remember that you aren't the only client for the broker, and the broker might be working with other clients at the same time. This means that you might not receive the full attention that you need to make things work out for you the right way. Calls might go unanswered, deals might fall through, and deadlines might go missed.

All in all, working with a broker makes things easy and fast for you. Take time to find the perfect broker for your needs so that you enjoy the benefits.

Banks and Real Estate Loans

The primary role of a bank in a real estate investment deal is to finance your investment. However, it has become increasingly difficult to find a bank that can bankroll your business. You have to submit document after document each day just to make things work out. The good news is that more and more banks are getting into real estate lending.

As an investor, especially one that has just jumped onto the real estate investment bandwagon, you need to have a quick way to get money. If the process is long, then you will end up losing deals to other investors with bigger financial muscles than you.

The Process of Getting a Bank Loan

If you think that looking for the ideal property to invest in is hard, then you haven't gone through the stress of being pre-approved for a loan. You need to bear in mind that the application process right from filling out the form to getting approved for the loan can take a minimum of 4 weeks. It is also harder to qualify for an investment loan compared to other types of loans such as car and home loans. The reason behind this is that banks and other financial institutions find investment properties having a higher risk than others.

The first step towards getting a loan is to get pre-approved. Preapproval involves filing an application and providing all the requirements. After you submit the information, you have to wait for 3-7 days to know whether you have been preapproved or your application has been denied.

The preapproval gives you a grace period of 6 months, during which time you need to look for properties. If you already have a property in mind, the bank uses independent valuers to evaluate it. The process of evaluation might take another 7 days.

What Do You Need to Qualify for a Bank Loan?

1. *Down Payment:* You need to pay some money, usually 20% of the property as a down payment. However, the bank doesn't restrict you to this value—you can pay more to improve the interest rates.
2. *A Good Credit Score*: Like any other application, you need to have a stellar credit score to apply for a loan. Banks usually need a score of 620 or more to consider your application. The credit score determines your creditworthiness—the ability to repay the loan on time. The higher the credit score, the better an interest rate you expect.
3. *Debt-to-Income Ratio:* This shows how much you have borrowed in the past in comparison to your earnings. The higher the DTI ratio, the lower the chances of

getting approved for a loan, so make sure the ratio is slow as possible.

4. *Cash Reserves:* Banks know that investment loans aren't a joke, and they are very strict when it comes to this aspect of lending. They are out to make sure that you can repay your loan. This is the reason they need you to have at least 6 months of mortgage payments in your account to qualify. This amount is on top of the money you put down as down payment.

Benefits of Bank Loans

Now that you have seen the various requirements to guarantee you a bank loan, what are the advantages that you enjoy when you opt for a bank loan?

- *You get to use other people's money.* With a bank loan, you get to use money from other people and save yours for other tasks. When using a bank loan, you only put up a certain percentage of your money to qualify but still enjoy the benefits of acquiring the whole property. You can use your money for other investments.
- *Low interest.* Most mortgages come with high-interest rates that are a barrier for most new investors, but when it comes to real estate loans, the interest rate is reasonable. This is true if you have a stellar credit score

to match. The low-interest rate helps you save a lot of money that you can use to handle other aspects of investing.

- *Grow your investment power.* With the use of the loan, you can easily increase the investment power. This allows you to purchase more and more property this way.
- *Quick approval.* As long as you meet the minimum requirements for the mortgage, you can easily qualify for the loan.

Disadvantages of Investment Loans

- *Tough to qualify.* For those investors with low credit scores, it can be a real hustle qualifying for the loan. The bank is careful to lend only to those businesses that show the promise of repaying the loan so that they cover any losses that might occur in the future.
- *High-interest rates.* For businesses just starting, you might find that the interest rate can be higher than what is comfortable for you. High-interest rates make it hard for you to expand because you know that, at the end of the day, you are spending a huge percentage of the profits on repaying the interest.

Private Real Estate Investment

One of the most important aspects of real estate investing is private real estate investments. The term refers to the practice of investing in assets that are managed by a third party, usually an investment manager. These acquisitions have many advantages:

- As an investor, you gain a lot from the experience that is provided by the private investor. The sponsor is usually an expert that comes with experience in real estate investing and who usually has operations run by professionals.
- When you go into private real estate investments, you usually know the cost of investments upfront as documented in the contracts.
- Diversification is possible because you can make the investments in a variety of sizes and asset types.
- As the investor, you don't have to handle the hands-on operation of the activities that are privy to the business.
- You also enjoy high returns on your investment.

Institutional vs. Retail Investments: What Is the Difference?

We have a wide range of real estate investors as you might know, with each category having its differences. Among these, some are considered institutional investors, while others are considered retail or non-institutional. Knowing the difference between the two makes it easy for you to handle your business much better.

Institutional Investor: These are the big players in the home and account for a huge volume of trades in the investment market. They move large blocks of properties and have a huge influence on how the market moves. These investors are subject to little regulations.

Due to the size of these investors, they can gain access to investments which most people cannot access.

Retail Investors: This is the normal investor that buys and sells properties via a broker. They don't invest for someone else but managing their funds.

Chapter : 6

Looking Into the Future

Real estate investing is just like any other business out there — you have to come up with the right goals or you are doomed to fail. Without goals, you have no definite purpose for yourself and your team. Let us look at the advantages of having goals in real estate investing.

What are Goals?

Goals refer to the resolutions that you come up with to achieve certain results. The goals might be short term or long term, depending on what you strive to accomplish.

You need to differentiate between goals and wishes. Wishes are desires, but goals are focused and specific with timelines. So, why should you have goals?

Goals help you to focus your attention and go ahead to achieve desirable outcomes. In a real estate investment business, one of the goals is profitability. However, remember that you won't make profits if you don't sell the property.

Additionally, employees look up to you to communicate to them what you expect of them, and goals give you the chance to give them this direction.

The goals also provide motivation for the employees since they know what they are working towards. You can also use the goals to plan for the course of action of the business. Once you achieve the goals, you can go ahead and celebrate.

Why Do You Need Goals?

1. *To measure success.* When setting the goals, you need to make sure they are measurable in such a way you can determine whether they meet the benchmark you have put down. You can compare the results of the business to the goals to see whether you met all objectives. With measurable objectives, you also have a chance to be competitive in a dynamic market.
2. *To promote cohesion.* When you set goals, you make sure that everyone in the team understands what ultimate prize is and why they are working towards it. When the team understands the need to work towards the goals, they understand why you make certain decisions, even if they don't resonate with them.

However, as a takeaway, you need to understand that it is not a guarantee that the goals will lead to the success of the organization. You are better off with goals than having none.

Now that we know why we need to set up goals, we want to go ahead and look at the various steps in coming up with goals the right way.

Steps to Come Up with Perfect Goals

1. *Understand why you are in real estate.* You might have all the resources, knowledge, the best team, and yet fail at real estate investing. Until you understand why you decided to get into real estate investing in the first place is when you will succeed at what you do.

So, before you can do anything else, it is vital that you understand what motivated you to get into this venture. Do you wish to make more money? Do you plan to leave your job and focus on investment? This is the first step towards setting the perfect goals.

2. *Make them realistic.* Now that you have understood the motivation behind the goal, the next thing is to come up with realistic goals. This means you have to be as specific as possible so that you set a clear goal as

opposed to general items. Make sure you write the goals down.

3. *Give them a timeline.* Successful investors have the option to set short-term and long-term goals. Short term goals are meant to be completed in a year or less. Short term goals then help you achieve the long term goals. These can be several years, for instance, 5 or 10.

4. *Commit to the goals.* Identifying and coming up with your goals is just a drop in the ocean when it comes to goal setting and implementation. The next part that is hard is making sure you implement these goals. Implementing the goals needs you to be disciplined, committed, and focused.

5. *Incorporate them in a business plan.* For you to succeed in real estate, you need to come up with a business plan. The plan outlines what you plan to accomplish and the various steps that you need to run to make it happen. The plan needs to have a definition of your market, the mission statement, the goals, strategies as well as expected issues that you might face.

6. *Identify a niche.* For your goals to work, you must intend to use them in a specific niche. When you identify a niche, you will get out the various strategies that aren't in line with your goals.

7. *Make your goals SMART.* Regardless of the type of goals that you set, you need to make sure that they are

SPECIFIC, MEASURABLE, ATTAINABLE, REALISTIC and TIMED. Make sure you review your goals regularly to make sure they are along these lines.

Barriers to Goal Setting for Investors

We have looked at the setting of the goals, but it comes a time when you meet challenges that make it hard for you to achieve these goals. These challenges include:

1. *Changing Real Estate Market:* This is why you need to evaluate your business goals each time and compare them with the market. The continual assessment has an impact on the strategy that you adopted when you started out so that you align them with your goals. Failure to align your goals with a changing market makes it hard for you to attain your goals.
2. *A Poor Decision-Making Process:* Sure, you might come up with the best goals, but if you can't match this with the right decision-making process, then the goals will fail miserably. If there is a decision that needs to be taken before a goal is completed, and then it gets blocked by the manager who has the authority to make the final decision, then the entire decision gets delayed.
3. *Lack of Enough Resources:* To accomplish a goal, you need to have all the resources you need in terms of

money, time, and labor. You need to have a person who will handle the various activities that lead to the goal getting completed while you need to have the time and money to fund the various requirements.

4. *Lack of Expectations:* Your goals need to have clear expectations that are measurable. Without a clear goal, your team fails to know what to do at what time.

5. *Putting Some Goals to Be More Vital Than Others:* Some investors place some goals to have more priority than others due to personal preferences. You need to achieve goals according to the timeline because you need to understand the goals that you come up with form a part of the whole process. Focus on achieving all the goals to make sure you don't leave any out.

6. *Setting Inappropriate Goals:* You need to set goals that are appropriate to the type of investment projects you run. They also need to consider various internal aspects such as the size, market share, financial condition, and many more. Goals might be inappropriate if you cannot attain them. Additionally, if you can't assess their value to the investment, then you need to modify them to suit your needs.

7. *A Complex Environment:* If the nature of your venture isn't friendly to the attainment of the goals, then you need to review your goals. Make sure the structure of the venture allows for the attainment of the goals.

8. *Reluctance to Have Goals:* Many investors are reluctant to come up with the right goals for their venture. This might be due to lack of skills, fear of failure, or just lack of the right attitude. An investor that avoids this level of accountability will deter any efforts towards achievement of the goals.

When you set your goals, you have the option of setting short-term or long term goals. Let us look at these two goals and what they entail.

Long-Term Versus Short-Term Goals

The goals you come up with have a definite time period that you attach to each of them. The shorter the goal, the more you have to put in to achieve it while the longer the goals, the more you have to spend to achieve it.

Short-Term Goals

Short-term goals, when it comes to real estate investing, refer to planning for less than three years. This is not a popular occurrence because many people opt for longer-term investment in real estate.

Many investors shy away from short-term investing because they don't have enough time to get reliable insight into the prospects of the project for providing returns in the future. Additionally, many lenders shy away from such investments because they find out that they can't trust the investor to guide the property through the full cycle.

Short-term investments require you to come up with goals that will last 3 years or less. One of the best short-term strategies is the rental market. Rentals are a good prospective because they allow you to return your money in the shortest time possible.

Short-term investment goals are ideal for properties that are in areas with stability in value. You also need to come up with these goals if you have substantial amounts of cash that you can devote to the development of the real estate as well as have access to professionals that are able to work to improve the price of your property in the shortest time possible.

On the flip side, a volatile market will destroy the short term goals. A short period of time might not be ideal for recovery in such a market.

A few short-term goals that you can set include:

- Joining a real estate investment club
- Finding the right broker that works with investors related to your niche

- Looking for a mentor to help you achieve success in the market
- Hiring a coach to help you with your investment
- Evaluating more than five houses each week.
- Revenue maximization

Long-Term Goals

On the other hand, long-term goals are meant to be achieved for periods that exceed 3 years. This makes the market to be stable and allows you to modify the goals according to the changes in the market.

As an investor, you need to come up with goals intended to last more than 10 years. However, to make this work for you, it is imperative that you have short-term milestones to evaluate the integrity of these goals.

Some of the long-term goals include:

- Expanding your clientele base
- Being more competitive than other investors in your circle
- Better media visibility
- Doubling of your annual profit

One of the benefits of long-term real estate goals is that you achieve greater things. For instance, if you decide to go for long-term investing, you seek to make a consistent positive cash flow that translates into better profits. After you come up with long-term goals, you have to go ahead and achieve them. This isn't as easy as it seems because you have to sacrifice a lot to get to these goals.

To achieve these goals and make them effective, you have to follow a few tips:

- *Connect the goals to your values.* When it comes to achieving long-term goals, you need to stick to the goals and match them to the core values of your business. Many times, we forget about the final outcome of the goals and instead focus on the motivation. To achieve the goals, try and connect them to your underlying values.
- *Break them into short-term goals.* You don't expect to go through the process of implementing your long-term goal in one big step. Every project that you have needs to be broken into smaller milestones so that you can get it done. Breaking your long-term goals into shorter tasks makes them manageable and more realistic. Make sure you do something each day towards the achievement of the goals.

Evaluation of Goals for Refinement and to Establish Effectiveness

Before we can look at how to evaluate your goals so that you can refine them, you need to understand that goals are the mainstay of any strategy. A strategy without goals is like a tour guide without a map — he will always guess the direction instead of knowing what direction to take next.

While it is exciting to come up with the best goals ever, you need to review them periodically and make sure you are always on the right path. You need to evaluate these goals time and again, but how frequent should this be?

The answer to the question is different for many people due to the circumstances and needs. However, regardless of the circumstances, different investors hit various milestones at the same time. Let us look at the various milestones in real estate investing:

- Coming up with an idea
- Setting the idea in motion
- Collecting enough capital
- Buying the first property
- Selling the first property
- Selling a number of properties

Make sure you set the evaluation period so that you match it to the milestones. The evaluation period can be in terms of months or years. However, make sure you don't make the period too long such that you lose track of the changes.

What is Evaluation?

Before we go ahead and look at the different phases of evaluation, we need to understand what evaluation means. This is an activity that reviews the performance of the different goals and whether the actions are intended to achieve the goals on time.

The evaluation, if well defined, will improve the quality of the investment proceeds to help you define the goals better and identify the important milestones as well as indicators of success. The information you glean from the reviews will give you what you need to make better decisions.

For evaluation to work, you need to come up with the best plan that you can. You have to understand what key metrics you are looking for and what each metric means to you.

Here are a few indicators that you should never ignore:

1. *Lead Generation Indicators:* You want to teach the number of people that you talk to each day. The contact can be a lead that has originated from you, the team or

an expert, and one that you have talked to. This indicator lets you know whether you have been attracting enough people in the pipeline to achieve the goals you wish to.

2. *Opportunity Indicators:* These indicators include meeting a first-time buyer to show them the property or make plans. Apart from the buyers, you also need to note down the number of sellers that you meet on a daily basis who are interested in your property. Once you have the metrics, you need to consider the conversion rates between these appointments. If you are contacting so many people but getting very few appointments, you need to change the approach, or you are targeting the wrong audience.

3. *Performance Indicators:* The first indicator to look at is the number of buyers that have identified you as their sole agent. You also need to look at the listing agreement, whereby you look at the sellers that have agreed to give you their property to sell. Make sure you know how many listings you receive before you get a purchase, which gives you an idea of the conversion rate. Apart from these indicators, you can go ahead and get your own from what your goals are.

4. *Average Income per Sale:* This is the amount that you get for each sale, totaled up and divided by the number of successful sales. When you have this metric, you get to

know well enough how profitable each of your transaction is.

5. *Number of Days on the Market:* This refers to the number of days that the property stays on the market before you close the deal. The average number of days will tell you whether the there is an issue with the home, that is, if the property stays on the market for too long, or tell you that the property is on high demand, that is, if it gets taken up faster than you can think.

6. *Number of Visits per Sale:* Here, we look at the average number of times that you show the property to the interested buyers before you sell the property. This metric helps define and monitor whether the price of the home is priced properly.

When it comes to these metrics, you get to know whether your goals are performing the right way or not.

When to Modify Your Goals

If you realize that the goals you came up with aren't performing the way you thought they would, you need to modify the goals so that you achieve more. Many investors decide to sell short and invest their time and efforts somewhere else, something that isn't a solution. While modifying goals can be a great idea, you need to be sure that the ones that you will come up with will be better than what you had before.

Let us look at the various issues that can make you modify your goals:

1. *Changes in circumstances.* When your financial goals change, you need to reflect this in writing. Additionally, you need to evaluate the investment portfolio and include everything that has happened in your journey the past few days and then make a decision. Look at your tax decision, the debt level, and many more.
2. *The level of risk tolerance.* If the timeline has changed, then you need to tweak your goals to reflect these changes. If you had short term investment plans and you decide to extend them to become long-term investments, then it becomes the right trigger to change the goals.
3. *You are losing out.* If you realize that you are underperforming in each transaction, then you need to change the goals so that you can adopt a better strategy that will give you profits.
4. *Changes in funds:* If you came up with short-term goals just because you had a limit to your funds, then it's time to change your goals to reflect the changes in the funding. You need to make sure the funds continue to

give you the support for your financial objectives and investment portfolio.

Return on Investment in Real Estate

The rate of return on investment refers to the returns you get when you invest in a property over a certain period. The ROI is calculated as a percentage of the investment. When the percentage is positive, it shows that you are making a profit from the investment; when the percentage is negative, it shows that you have been losing money on the investment.

To get this return, you need to take the cost of investment and divide it with the cost of the investment, and then you multiply the result by 100 to get the percentage.

So, how can you use the rate to take your business to another level? Well, you can compare this value to the average rate of return in the market which tells you whether you are below the average or above average.

If you find that the percentage is way below the average, you need to reevaluate your goals and then modify them.

How to Evaluate the Performance

Before you can come up with this value, you need to look at various aspects:

- *Understand the statements of accounts.* The statement of accounts gives you a structure of the performance, including how much value you can attribute to the account.
- *Include the costs.* Before you can come up with the percentage, you need to make sure that you factor in any expenses that you have incurred. You also need to factor in the fees that you paid when selling the property.
- *Role of taxes.* Taxes affect the way you earn your interest. Make sure you deduct the taxes from the rate of return so that you know you know the ideal ROI.
- *Look at the inflation.* If you plan to buy and hold on to the property for the long term, you need to look at the inflation in the market at the moment. Inflation refers to the loss of value of currency over time. Make sure you subtract the inflation rate from the cost to come up with the right rate of return.

As you can see, long-term investment is the way to go if you plan to make money and enjoy your investment. However, you have to make a lot of sacrifices that include sacrificing quick returns on investments. Make sure you make your results as well as earnings exponential.

Chapter : 7
Understanding Real Estate Investment Risks and Risk Management

As an investor, you have to understand that there are various risks that come with real estate investment. However, just like any other asset, the higher the risks, the higher is the potential of making profits.

Risks in Real Estate Investment

1. **General Market Risks**: All the markets in any part of the world come with various risks that are tied to various trends. These trends include a failing economy, inflation, interest rates, and more. While you can try and eliminate a few of the shocks that hit the market, some will affect you.
2. **Idiosyncratic Risk:** This is related to a specific property category. In this type of risk, the higher the risk, and the higher the potential to make more returns. Adding a new block to an existing property will limit the capacity for you to collect the rent on the property during the time you are handling the renovations.

Another common example is when you start developing a property from the ground up because you tend to take on more risk than just the aspect of construction. When building a property from the ground up, you will have to face the risk of government agencies not providing the necessary approvals that will allow the project to move forward.

Another type of risk occurs when you decide to buy a property that is surrounded by empty lots. The risk of another building cropping up next to the property you have bought and blocking your view is a high possibility and a risk at that.

3. **Risk of Creditworthy:** You need to understand how stable the property's income stream is. Remember the amount you make as rental income is what eventually drives the value of the house. Some companies will pay you more to lease your apartment compared to others. However, you need to note that even the best clients that you regard to be highly creditworthy might end up going bankrupt.
4. **Liquidity Risk:** When you go to the market, you look at various things that include how liquid the market is. You need to look at whether the market will still give you the business you need and whether you have an exit strategy for the market before you pick an asset. Some markets are evergreen, with buyers available the year round, while in other markets you get a nearly

equal number of market participants, which makes it easy to get a deal but hard to get out.

5 **Replacement Cost Risk:** As the need for more space on the market causes leases to skyrocket in older properties, you need to realize that it will take such a short time for the attractive rates to bring about new buildings and lead to supply risk. For instance, a nearby new high-rise building can make your property to become obsolete due to providing better facilities going at lower rents. Many times, you might think of raising rents to compete, but this might lead to loss of tenants.

6 **Leverage Risk:** The higher the debt you command on an investment, the higher the risk that you face. If you have a huge debt, you need to expect more money from the project. However, this is not always the case, and you might find that the returns on your investment don't cover the repayments. The result is that you lose a lot of money on investments.

So, what we are implying is that you need to inquire about the various risks in any investment and then come up with the right investment decision. Don't go for an investment that doesn't make the risks clear.

Why Is Real Estate Risk More Complicated Than Other Asset Classes?

There are many reasons why risks in real estate investments are more complicated.

- The inherent money-time dimensions of the market and the inefficiency
- The capital intensity and vulnerable nature of the assets in question
- The vulnerability of real estate property to impact by external forces

Causes of Risk in Real Estate Investment

There are so many factors that can lead to real estate risks, and getting a grasp on them can be a huge challenge. Here are some of them:

1. **Information Analysis.** This is one of the risks that cannot be phased out of any property deal. The only thing you can do is to manage it so that you reduce its effect on the results. You can choose to minimize it or compensate it with another type of return. This risk can come up as a result of various causes:
- *Inaccurate and inconsistent data.* You rely on various reports to get the data on property values. While the

sources for these data try to verify it, there is no sure way to determine how accurate the data is. The only thing you can do to mitigate this factor is to try and understand how the data has been acquired, compiled, and what has been put down to avoid the various biases.

- *Lack of adequate information.* The real estate market is competitive, and any source of information is a closely guarded secret that even the best vendor will not reveal to you. So, what source of information should you deem verifiable? Fee-based vendors charge you a small fee to give you data that is better than other sources. Additionally, try to go for commercial brokers that have made a name on the market.

- *Failure to understand the fundamentals of the market.* Real estate is an asset class which comes with a set of distinguishing features that make it different from other industries. The property classes on the market are in a constant evolution that is as a result of environmental and static elements on the market. Additionally, the decisions on the market are made by individuals that have the sole responsibility of making sure the market runs smoothly. The biggest risk in such a situation is the failure to understand what happens in the market at all times.

2. **Unforeseen Changes in the Market.** There are a set of changes that you won't foresee at all when it comes to real estate trading including:

- *Unexpected regulations.* The government tends to change the regulations for real estate time and again, making it a volatile form of asset. You also need to know that the rules and regulations change from one state to another or even from one city to another.
- *The variation in the competitive environment.* If you have been keen, then you know that the current properties that were constructed 5 years ago aren't the same as those that were constructed 30 years ago. The emergence of technology has changed the way people perceive the market, and you will realize that competition comes in a completely different way.

Risk Management Process in Real Estate Investments

You cannot eliminate the risks from any asset category—all you can do is to compensate for the risk or minimize it. The process is simple and straightforward: identify an existing risk, manage the risk, and then evaluate the results to see whether you were successful or not. The process might be different depending on the kind of asset that is under scrutiny, but generally, the process remains the same.

There are a few ways that you can approach risk in the real estate realm, with some of the methods designed to reduce the risk, constraining the risk or compensate the loss that the risk has caused. Let us look at these various strategies.

Putting a Cap on Risks:

- *Avoiding the asset class.* Here, you manage the risk by avoiding a risky asset class due to its uncertainty and complexity.
- *Diversification.* When you diversify your investment portfolio, you end up with several properties in different classes so that you mitigate the risk that might be inherent in a single class. With various properties having different values, you stand to dampen any risks that come with holding on a single property.
- *Insurance.* There are some risks that you cannot anticipate, and when this happens, you need to manage them by shifting the burden of the risk to a third party through insurance. Consider the various types of insurance after you consider the possibility of the risk.
- *Use Contracts.* You can pass part of the risks to a third party through contracts that you manage.
- *Use Partnerships.* Using partnerships spreads the risk across more than one person so that you don't have to

shoulder the risks all by yourself. However, remember that having a partner can itself be a risk because some partners don't know what they are after.

Risk Reduction

- *Forecast Improvement.* Here, you develop better forecasts by using key indicators when making decisions. You can have better forecasts when you use both qualitative and quantitative insights into the structure of the market.
- *Opt for Reliable Models.* Due to the complex nature of real estate investments, you can improve the forecasts by using valid and reliable scientific methods. Make sure the models have both qualitative and behavioral elements.
- *Understand the Market Better.* When you understand the market better, you reduce the level of uncertainty that is a premise for most investors. Understand what drives value, factors that affect utilization, external forces, and their effects as well as market cycles.
- *Improve Data.* If your vendor isn't giving you the right information to allow you to make informed decisions, you need to change the vendor and find another. The data that the vendor returns should give you a wide view of the market while allowing you to make specific

decisions. You need to focus your attention on the main factors that have a huge impact on real market data so that you avoid data overload and confusion that might be a result of excess data.

- *Use Experience.* While data might be a great way to make conclusions on the market, you also need to use the experience you have gained over time to make decisions

Real Estate Taxes

One of the best ways to develop wealth and grow your cash flow is to invest in real estate. Apart from this, you can also enjoy some tax benefits. By leveraging the different benefits that tax provides, you can break even faster. Let us look at the various tax benefits that you gain.

- *Lower Tax Rate.* If you invest for the long term in real estate, the profit you make on a sale falls under long-term gains. These attract a low tax rate ranging from 0%-20% depending on the amount of returns. However, for those investing in short term deals, you won't be able to enjoy any tax benefits
- *The Value in Depreciation.* Real estate is like any other property—it loses value over time. Due to this, you can claim depreciation on the property. This means you

can depreciate the structure while depreciating the property value.

- *Refinancing Benefits.* By refinancing the property, you can improve cash flow. Some refinance options reduce the amount of mortgage you pay out.
- *Not Considered Real Business.* The IRA doesn't take real estate to be a business, so they take it that you don't earn any income from a property sale.
- *Deductions.* The best advantage that comes with real estate is in the form of deductions. Deductions are usually focused on rental properties. This means as an investor, you can deduct expenses you incur for conserving, managing, and maintaining the property in question.

One of the top deductions is the repair of the property. Since these repairs are aimed at making the property more livable, it doesn't add any value to your property so you can write off these deductions.

You can also deduct interest on the mortgage on primary residences. If you use your home office as your investment platform, then you can also deduct the costs of the non-office activities. Make sure you understand the various aspects of investing that you can deduct before you submit your returns.

- *Make Use of Flipping to Avoid Payment of Taxes.* What if you decide to avoid the capital gains? Well, you can work with flipping, whereby you buy the property then move it immediately to another owner.

After looking at these aspects of tax for real estate investments, the next thing to look at is the various mistakes that real estate investors make concerning taxation.

Real Estate Tax Assessment

Before you place a property on the market, you need to have an appraiser to evaluate them and determine their value. This value is the value of the property on the market. To determine this, you need to consider the size, the age, and the prior value of the property.

The appraiser also looks at the value of the house in relation to the value of other houses in the area.

The tax you pay is also determined by the assessment rates that are put in place by the government. However, you need to realize that values vary from jurisdiction to jurisdiction. The taxes you pay are a value that is a percentage of the results of the assessed value.

These taxes remain similar through the years but might at times change if you make any improvements on the property, such as adding an extension before you sell it off.

You can make money out of taxes if you are keen enough. For instance, if there are delinquent property taxes that have been sitting for several years, then the county can sell it off to recover the taxes.

Top Tax Mistakes That You Need to Avoid

1. *Reporting your income in a terrible way.* More than 75% of real estate investors don't know how to report the various categories of income. If you find that you have an issue with reporting your income, work with a tax planner that will help you change how you report your taxes each year. Planners help you save on taxes each year.
2. *Failure to take advantage of new tax laws.* New tax laws change the way you regard taxes as an investor. You need to make sure you understand what these changes are and how they affect your reporting. Make sure you understand what category you fall in when you report the taxes so that you understand what you are responsible for.

3. *Most investors fail to maximize their deductions.* Many investors aren't privy with the various details of deductions—they don't know when and how the deductions need to happen. Due to this, they end up failing to capitalize on the deductions, especially the home office deductions. To make use of this deduction, make sure you document how you use the office the best way.
4. *Wrong depreciation calculations.* You need to understand how to calculate depreciation on the property so that you understand how the IRS will calculate gains. Depreciation is the cost that you deduct in a different year than the one the cost was incurred. You need to capitalize on the calculations based on the kind of property you handle.
5. *Lack of proper record keeping.* Many investors miss out on deductions just because they were not able to keep good records. If you fall into this category, make sure that you have separate bank accounts to pay business expenses so that you track them the best way. Having all the expenses in front of you will help you determine what is deductible and what isn't. It also tells you to what extent the expenses are deductible.

With the mistake in perspective, you can easily rectify them so that you have a better experience with your taxes as an investor.

Are Your Real Estate Assets Protected?

Do you know that if your tenants or other interested parties sue you, it will be hard for you to protect the assets that are held in your names such as the name, business, and personal property? Well, due to this, you need to make sure you protect your assets to a huge extent. Here are the various ways this is possible:

1. *Segregate your assets.* If you own multiple properties that you plan to let go of, later on, you need to make sure you place them in separate legal segregates. The segregations depend on the different types of activities and the level of risk involved as well as how much each asset is valued at.
2. *Manage the assets using professionals.* You need to make sure that you assign the assets to professionals that will manage them on your behalf. Doing this makes it easy for you to protect the asset while you enjoy the tax benefits.
3. *Have good business practices.* For you to enjoy enhanced protection of your assets, you need to make sure you

maintain good business practices. These practices include following the regulations that are set down by each state or country, for instance, following the tight path towards buying and selling of property.

4. *Have correct titles.* Each property has a title associated with it that identifies the number, the size, the owner, and other information regarding the property. Without the title, you don't have what it takes to claim ownership of the property. To make sure you are protected at all times, make sure you have valid titles at all times. The title should also state the type of ownership of the property.

5. *Insure the property.* Insurance veils you and the tenants so that you are ready for any eventuality that comes your way.

6. *Avoid stupid things.* One of the easiest ways to lose the protection that you have is to commit a stupid act of negligence or defraud someone. When it comes to these acts, your insurance won't protect you in any way.

Bonus Chapter
Preface to the 3rd book "Potential of Real Estate Rentals

In the next book in this series, you will understand the power of passive income that you get from rent. You will understand the power of compound interest.

Go ahead to read about the different types of rental income in real estate investment.

After reading the book, you will be able to integrate an opportunity into the real estate strategy, the way it is mentioned in *Get Your Real Estate Strategies for Your Real Estate Life*.

Made in the USA
Coppell, TX
18 March 2020